SOCIAL SCIENCE RESEARCH ON BUSINESS:

PRODUCT AND POTENTIAL

SOCIAL SCIENCE RESEARCH ON BUSINESS: PRODUCT AND POTENTIAL

ROBERT A. DAHL

MASON HAIRE

PAUL F. LAZARSFELD

NEW YORK CITY · 1959

COLUMBIA UNIVERSITY PRESS

FOREWORD

Since its inception in 1954, the Ford Foundation's Program in Economic Development and Administration has had as one of its major interests the support of promising developments in higher education for business. One area in which fruitful developments have occurred recently is the application of methodology and analysis from the social sciences, including particularly, psychology, sociology, and political science, to the study of business problems.

To stimulate increased interest in the world of business as a subject for research by social scientists, and to encourage a greater appreciation on the part of faculty members in business administration of the potential contribution these underlying disciplines offer, the Foundation initiated a special, multi-phase program in 1958. In one phase of this program ten professors in graduate faculties of sociology, psychology, and political science, whose research interests are oriented toward problems of business, were selected for "master-fellowship" grants. The major portion of each five-year fellowship is designated for grants by the professor in support of doctoral candidates working on dissertations which bear upon business problems. Over the next five years it is expected that at least fifty young PH.DS in these social science fields will have done such dissertation research.

In a second phase of this program fellowships have been established to enable a select number of business administration faculty members to spend a full year pursuing a self-defined course of study in the social sciences (other than economics, which needs no such encouragement), statistics, or mathematics. Preference is being given to faculty members involved in imaginative research or in the development of new teaching materials, courses, and curricula. A number of fellowships are also being offered to members of sociology, anthropology, psychology, and political science faculties to enable them to spend a year engaged in research that applies the analytical tools of their disciplines to the study of the internal or external relationships of business firms.

A third phase of the special program has made three-year visiting professorships in the social sciences, applied mathematics, and statistics available to five selected schools of business administration.

A national dissertation competition has been established as the fourth phase. Outstanding doctoral dissertations on subjects bearing upon business problems will be selected and published. Candidates may be completing their doctorate as graduate students in business or in other fields relevant to the study of business.

The essays presented in this book constitute the final phase of the program. To broaden interest in and awareness of developments in the social sciences that may have application to the study of business, Professors Dahl, Haire, and Lazarsfeld were requested to write essays on the application of research in their respective disciplines—actual and potential—to business problems. Earlier versions of these essays appeared in professional journals. They have already aroused an enthusiastic response among social science and business administration faculty members. This volume was planned in the belief that the essays should be made more readily available to graduate students and faculty engaged in research and to interested members of the business community. The three contributions were written independently by the authors and do not necessarily represent the views of the Ford Foundation. It is hoped that this publication of them will further stimulate the discussions and re-thinking now current on the role of the various social sciences in the study of one of the most important institutions of modern society. As the essays attest, the study of business can be an exciting arena for the researcher.

Although progress has been made in the last fifteen years, the research surveyed in this volume has raised as many new and intriguing questions as it has answered. Much remains to be done. If the multiphase program described above should encourage new and fruitful developments, it shall have been successful.

Thomas H. Carroll
Vice President
The Ford Foundation

New York, New York
July 15, 1959

PREFACE

THE BUSINESS FIRM is one of the dominant institutions of modern life, not only in the United States but throughout much of the world. One may approve of the activities and organization of business, or deplore them, or look on with judicious resignation, but no thoughtful person will deny the *importance* of business in the contemporary world. And the importance of business is a sufficient reason why social scientists should study it.

In the three essays that follow, the authors do not attempt to appraise business but only to examine it. The essays reflect the conviction that whatever conclusions we might come to if we sought to evaluate the desirability of business (and there is no reason to suppose we would all agree), as social scientists we can not withdraw from the attempt to *understand* this critical aspect of modern life.

These essays were written at the request of the Ford Foundation as part of a broad program designed both to stimulate greater interest among political scientists, psychologists, and sociologists in the business firm as a subject of research, and to make students of management and business administration more aware of the potential contribution of these underlying social science disciplines to an understanding of business behavior[1].

This monograph is directed, therefore, to these two audiences: colleagues in our own disciplines, and teachers and students of business. We have tried to keep in mind the reader looking for a quick survey of what has been done by writers in each of these areas of the social

[1] Earlier versions of these essays appeared in professional journals; in their present form they have been somewhat expanded and integrated, and an annotated bibliography of select items has been appended. See Robert A. Dahl, "Business and Politics: A Critical Appraisal of Political Science," *American Political Science Review*, LIII (March, 1959), 1-34; Mason Haire, "Psychological Research Problems Relevant to Business and Industry," *Psychological Bulletin*, Vol. 56, No. 3, May 1959, pp. 169-194; Paul F. Lazarsfeld," Reflectionson Business; Consumers and Managers," *American Journal of Sociology*, LXV (The University of Chicago Press, July, 1959, Copyright 1959 by The University of Chicago), 1-31.

sciences, the young scholar interested in the possibilities of research on business, teachers in need of a summary or references to works in the field, and the student training for a career in business.

Naturally in short articles by three different authors writing from three different perspectives much has been left out that might have been covered and things have been included that a different trio of social scientists might have excluded. There are, in fact, some quite unexpected transpositions of perspectives. Thus it is the sociologist (Lazarsfeld) and not the psychologist (Haire) who concerns himself mainly with the analysis of *individual decisions* of consumers and businessmen. It is the political scientist (Dahl) and not the sociologist who examines the *structural* aspects of business as orders or systems. And it is Haire, the psychologist, rather than the political scientist or the sociologist, who focuses on the *conditions of efficiency* in the business enterprise.

It would not be difficult to imagine each writer assuming the perspective of one of the others rather than his own. But in each case, the choice was a result of a reflection on the particular contributions, past and potential, of the man's own field. None of the three essays is anything like a comprehensive survey of what has been or might be done on the study of business by students of that particular discipline. For example, Lazarsfeld has excluded the enormous volume of material that falls under the heading of industrial sociology. Dahl has deliberately left out the one aspect of business—governmental regulation—most extensively written about and studied by political scientists. Haire has not tried to cover the psychology of decision-making. In each case the reasons were much the same: in short essays it seemed more useful to stress some of the neglected areas of study and research than to cover topics on which there are a number of good textbooks.

We could have sought a nice fit where a topic in one essay was touched on in another. Instead, to illustrate with one example, where Lazarsfeld develops some highly specialized categories for describing motivations, Haire treats this in more theoretical terms, and Dahl in his one allusion to motives deliberately leaves the term undefined. The fact is, we were less concerned with writing a highly integrated book, in which each chapter reached out for unity with the others, than to reveal the richness of business as a subject for social research and the capacity of the social sciences to unearth these riches.

Because we indicate places where prospecting might bring large returns but do not spell out methods in any detail, it might be useful to say a word about one problem that will occur at once to any student of business: the problem of access to the business firm. Surely it is no accident that we know very much more about consumers than about business executives. It is not difficult to persuade businessmen that they would be better off if they knew more about consumers, nor to overcome the resistance of consumers themselves (who after all usually have no particular reason for concealing their preferences or their buying habits). But it is quite another matter to persuade businessmen that they themselves should be studied. They may feel that what they do not know about themselves can not be important; and from their point of view there are important disadvantages in working under the microscope of a social scientist whose avid curiosity is both time-consuming and potentially embarrassing. Moreover, there are sheer problems of scale. It could cost about as much in research funds, time, and effort to study some aspect of managerial behavior in ten business firms as to survey 2,000 consumers. And what are we to do with a sample of executives from ten firms?

There is no easy answer to these problems. We can not provide one here. But an encouraging number of experiences indicate that the problems, though difficult, are by no means insurmountable. The gaps in our knowledge about business and businessmen can not be explained entirely or even chiefly on the grounds of difficulties in access. The *big* gaps seem to result from the fact that we have not tried, or because of some general obstacle in our theories or methods that is not peculiar to the study of business but to the state of the discipline.

We think the attempt to overcome these difficulties is important, not only because the social sciences can ill afford to neglect such a significant area of human activity but also for social policy. As we said at the outset, these essays examine business but they do not appraise it. The task of appraisal is a very large one; and we can not judge intelligently without the kinds of knowledge emphasized in these essays. Nonetheless, the attempt to judge business enterprise and its consequences, to place it in some framework of goals and values, and to observe it in the perspective of the power relations and morality of our social structure—indeed of our whole civilization—is an effort fully as essential as anything we have urged in this book.

R. A. D.
M. H.
P. F. L.

CONTENTS

BY ROBERT A. DAHL

Business and Politics:

A Critical Appraisal of

Political Science

For all the talk and all the public curiosity about the relations between business and politics, there is a remarkable dearth of studies on the subject. What *is* written is more likely to come from the pen of a sociologist, an historian, a lawyer, or an economist than from a political scientist. One would suppose that the role of business, particularly big business, in the political system would be a matter of central concern to political scientists. And so it may be. But with a few exceptions those who write about it are men like Adolph Berle, a lawyer, C. Wright Mills, a sociologist, and Robert Brady, an economist.

Introduction

Lest it be thought that I have over-stated the point, here is some supporting evidence. During the past fifty years, only about a dozen articles have appeared on the subject of business in the pages of *The American Political Science Review*. In his analysis of articles published in the five general political science journals of this country during the years 1925–29, 1939–41, and 1952–54, Waldo found no articles at all on business in the first period, only two articles in the second, and only nine in the third.[1] If we look at proposed doctoral dissertations, the output is not great. Out of the many thousand dissertation titles

[1] The three periods are his. Some additional articles may be concealed under other headings, such as "politics, parties, and pressure groups." Dwight Waldo, *Political Science in the United States of America, A Trend Report* (Paris, UNESCO, 1956), p. 39.

listed in *The American Political Science Review* in the past 15 years, only 75 deal in any way with business.

When political scientists do take up their pens to write about business, the chances are that they will concern themselves with the relatively well established field of government regulation in the broad sense. For example, among the 75 dissertation titles there were twice as many in the area of government regulation, control, and administration as in the next most popular field, politics, parties, pressure groups, and propaganda.

TABLE 1

Proposed Dissertations in Political Science Dealing with Business and Politics, 1942–1958, Classified According to Some of the Conventional Areas of Political Science

	U.S.	FOREIGN	TOTAL
AREA	N	N	N
Government regulation, admin. & control	18	10	28
Politics, parties, pressures, propaganda	10	3	13
International Relations			
Law: 4			
Politics: 4	⋆	⋆	8
Personnel, labor, coll. bargaining	7	—	7
Public policy (assessment)	6	—	6
Public law	5	—	5
Political thought, ideologies	2	—	2
Other	⋆	⋆	2
Unclassified	⋆	⋆	4
Totals	48	13	75

⋆ Total not properly classifiable in either category.

Doubtless there are many reasons for the paucity of articles and books by political scientists on this topic: traditional conceptions of the subject matter of political science, unfamiliarity with available materials, difficulties in research, and lack of relevant theories to guide research. I am not going to argue that we should all shift our attention forthwith; but I do intend to show that there are some extremely interesting and important topics with varying degrees of relevance to political science as the field is usually defined, to which the political scientist might, with his skills and interests, profitably direct his attention. In this essay, I propose to make a brief survey of the state of our knowledge with respect to four questions:

I. What kinds of political orders are constituted by relations within business firms? How do the orders operate?

II. What kind of a political order is constituted by the relations among business firms? How does the order operate?

III. What are the relations between business and the American political order? (I will also consider under this head some of the relations of American business to international politics.)

IV. What are the general consequences for the political order of the present organization of business in the United States? And conversely? (I will consider under this heading some rather more general questions than those considered under III.)

You will notice that, judged by the usual preoccupations of political scientists, we shall move from the less familiar to the more familiar. Hardly any studies by political scientists bear directly on the first two questions. For that matter, not many deal with the last two either; but these questions, and particularly the fourth, are evidently regarded by most political scientists as relevant to the "discipline." It may be debatable whether "political science" should or should not encompass the first two topics, but I propose to avoid this arid enterprise and content myself instead with indicating briefly how these matters are germane to our understanding of political orders and processes.

The Business Firm As A Political Order

A business firm, like a trade union, religious organization, or state, has a political order. Like the internal "government" of the economic system, the internal government of the firm has been effectively proscribed to the economic theorist and ignored by the political scientist. The "theory of the firm," which has occupied a vast amount of attention among economists, has little to say, except implicitly, about questions of power, influence, sanctions, legitimacy—in short, government.

A number of political theorists have stressed the value of studying the political orders of social organizations other than the state.[2] Most recently, Bertrand de Jouvenel, who is occupied with some of the most ancient, persistent, and imperative problems of political theory, has argued:

One of the obstructions which has hitherto hindered the development of political science was its limitation to the aggregates called States, which are too long-lived for any summary comprehension of them to be possible. Just as genetics has greatly gained by the study of heredity as it operates over many generations of short-lived insects, so political science will gain greatly from an ability to work on aggregates that mature quickly; of these, life in society presents instances all around us.[3]

The most explicit exponent of the view that the firm or business enterprise is worth studying as a governmental institution is probably Peter Drucker, who brought to the study of business firms a well established interest in political theory.[4] Aside from his enthusiastic

---

[2] On this point, as on many others, Charles Merriam had many insights and suggestions; e.g., see his *Public and Private Government* (New Haven, 1944). A number of political scientists have examined the internal government of private organizations, though they have not usually paid much attention to the business firm as such. The studies are too numerous to cite here, but of seminal influence are O. Garceau, *The Political Life of the A.M.A.* (Cambridge, 1941) and D. Truman, *The Governmental Process* (New York, 1951), Part 2. For a recent essay, see G. McConnell, "The Spirit of Private Government," *The American Political Science Review*, Vol. 52 (September, 1958), pp. 754–70.

[3] *Sovereignty, An Inquiry into the Political Good* (Chicago, 1957), p. 25.

[4] E.g., P. F. Drucker, *The New Society, the Anatomy of the Industrial Order* (New York, 1949), p. 44 and *passim*. In 1943, Drucker—then teaching political theory at Bennington College —was invited by General Motors "to study and to report on its managerial policies and organization from the standpoint of an outside consultant, in which capacity (he) served for eighteen months." Out of this experience came *The Concept of the Corporation* (New York, 1946), from which the quotation is taken, at page viii. Most recently, he has written a kind of handbook for executives, *The Practise of Management* (New York, 1954). His first book, *The End of Economic Man* (London, 1940), was, despite the title, essentially a work in political theory, for it was an analysis of the rise of irrational behavior in the form of totalitarianism.

description of the organization of General Motors in *The Concept of the Corporation,* there are remarkably few concrete studies. The most extensive is undoubtedly *Business Leadership in the Large Corporation,* by R. A. Gordon, who pursued a method of analysis with which the political scientist will find little to disagree:

In a system of delegated power such as is found in the large corporation an analysis of business leadership must deal with three related problems, two of them connected with the process of decision-making. First, where do important business decisions originate? . . . Second, what other persons, if any, veto or approve decisions? . . . Finally, with whom is lodged the coordinating authority for the enterprise as a whole . . .?[5]

For nearly half a century, observers have called attention to the discrepancy between the formal-legal structure of government in large business corporations and their real constitutions. In the formal-legal structure, control over decisions is a function of ownership. But as early as 1913 the Pujo Committee of the House of Representatives noted that in large corporations with numerous and widely scattered stockholders, "the management is virtually self-perpetuating and is able through the power of patronage, the indifference of stockholders, and other influences to control a majority of the stock."[6] The Committee, which was mainly interested in the influence of bankers, went on to point out that "where representatives of a great banking house are on the board and are financing the corporation and in close relations with the management the policy of the corporation is largely determined by the bankers where they choose to assume that responsibility." This view of the locus of power in the corporation was a dominant one until quite recently. In 1927 it was reiterated by William Z. Ripley, a professor of political economy at Harvard, in his *Main Street and Wall Street.*[7] Meanwhile, A. A. Berle, then a young member of the New York bar, had been developing a parallel but more comprehensive argument in journal articles; the book he subsequently

[5] Washington, 1945, pp. 57–58.

[6] U. S. Congress, House of Representatives, Report of the Committee Appointed Pursuant to House Resolutions 429 and 504 to Investigate the Concentration of Control of Money and Credit, 62d Congress, 2d Session, February 28, 1913, p. 147.

[7] New York, 1927, ch. 4 and *passim.*

wrote with Gardner Means, an economist, has long since taken its place as one of the minor classics of social analysis.[8]

Gordon's study, however, marks an important refinement in the evolution of these interpretations, for where the earlier works had stressed the domination of directors and management over stock-holders, or of bankers over directors and management, Gordon showed that control over decisions had come to rest even more narrowly: with management. Not only do chief executives generally dominate over their boards of directors, even to the point where executives select their own directors rather than the other way around; but the process of bureaucratization has gone so far, in Gordon's view, that on many important questions the final decisions do not even lie with the chief executives but with the professional bureauc-racies of the corporation. Gordon also found that: 1) Salaried execu-tives make up a large proportion of the membership of boards of directors of their own companies. (On 35 of 155 giant corporations analysed, executives constituted at least 50 per cent of the board.) 2) In contrast to the earlier findings of the Pujo committee, the im-portance of outside influences such as bankers and minority blocks of stockholdings had dwindled relatively, in part because of the greater availability of other sources of corporate capital, but in part also because of the high degree of professionalization and executive au-tonomy in the government of the corporation. And 3) committee decision-making had grown, while the old-fashioned lone-wolf entrepreneurial figure had all but disappeared.[9]

Although there have been no subsequent studies as extensive and careful as Gordon's, some corroborative material exists. In 1953 T. K. Quinn, a one-time vice president of General Electric, wrote a volume of reminiscences and observations valuable chiefly because Quinn is one of the very few "insiders" who have been moved to write critically about their own firms. On the subject of directors, he wrote:

In General Electric the election of directors was only formalized at stockholders' meetings. The directors were in every case selected by the officers, who in turn

---

[8] *The Modern Corporation and Private Property* (New York, 1932).

[9] Gordon, *op. cit.*, pp. 71–73, 75–77, 80–81, 91, 99, 105–107, 119, 122, 131–35.

always voted to perpetuate the officers. We had then, in effect, a huge economic state governed by nonelected, self-perpetuating officers and directors —the direct opposite of the democratic method. I am not condemning anyone but simply explaining a system, quite generally effective, which has grown up around us.

The fewer the men in control of a giant corporation, the narrower the field of selection for officers and directors. I recall a discussion with the President of General Electric one time when one of our directors had resigned and another had died. There were two vacancies to fill, and the question was whom to "elect." The selections were finally made largely on the basis of appearances. We did consider how helpful they might be in influencing business our way, but in general what was wanted was a board that would look well on paper. So far as the operation of the business was concerned, they were mere figureheads anyway. Vice-presidents, who were supposed to be elected by the board of directors, were always named by the President. In every instance the figurehead board were "good boys" and endorsed the selections with their votes.[10]

In 1947, M. T. Copeland and A. Towl of the Harvard Graduate School of Business wrote a volume that emphasized, far more than Gordon had, the importance of the directors. But a careful reading of their book suggests that the influence on decisions that directors *should* and might exert (in the view of the authors) is very different from what they actually *do* exert. For their case studies indicate that it is mainly when a chief executive dies without having chosen a successor, or when the corporation is in a severe crisis, that directors can successfully interpose their influence; or for that matter are even disposed to.[11]

Gordon's view of the government of the large corporation suggests some highly significant questions. First, there is the empirical question whether many large corporations actually approximate his description. Berle evidently continues to adhere to his earlier view that control over any decision lies mainly with the directors.[12]

---

[10] T. K. Quinn, *Giant Business: Threat to Democracy* (New York, 1953) p. 145.

[11] M. T. Copeland and A. Towl, *The Board of Directors and Business Management* (Boston, 1947), esp. pp. 33–36, 43–43, 52–57, 65–66, and 71–72.

[12] "The control system in today's corporations, when it does not lie solely in the directors as in the American Telephone and Telegraph Company, lies in a combination of the directors of a so-called control bloc (a misnomer, incidentally) plus the directors themselves. For practical purposes, therefore, the control or power element in most large corporations rests in its group of directors and it is autonomous —or autonomous if taken together with a control bloc. And inheritance-tax distribution of

Second, on either view the existence of such a high degree of autonomy in corporate decisions poses serious problems of public policy. Are the controls over the corporation exerted through the operation of the price system adequate, or should they be supplemented by additional controls of some sort? The answer will depend in part, of course, upon one's assessment of the strength of price system controls; and here the relevance of the classic competitive model is dubious — yet there seems to be no useful alternative model. If one were to opt for additional public controls, what would be necessary to make these controls effective? Here one's answer might depend on whether one accepts Gordon's view or Berle's. On either view, the belief that the "power" of businessmen would be tamed by professionalization of business management, which seemed so hopeful to critics as various as Tawney, Brandeis, and Follett, is scarcely justified; for with a speed that these reformers could hardly have anticipated, professionalization is being achieved. But if the means they advocated are now commonplace, it is doubtful whether Tawney and Brandeis would agree that the *ends* they were seeking by professionalization have been reached.[13]

In the third place, the governmental structure of the modern corporation as viewed by Gordon has some remarkable parallels (and some

stock being what it is, the trend is increasingly to management autonomy. This is a self-perpetuating oligarchy." *Economic Power and the Free Society, A Preliminary Discussion of the Corporation* (The Fund for the Republic, New York, 1958), p. 10. Berle's pamphlet is one of three published so far under the auspices of the Fund for the Republic and its panel of consultants — of whom Berle is one — on "The Problems of the Free Society." The other pamphlets are: Scott Buchanan (also a consultant), *The Corporation and the Republic* (New York, 1958), and Andrew Hacker, *Politics and the Corporation* (New York, 1958).

[13] To a remarkable degree, the objectives set out by R. H. Tawney in *The Acquisitive Society* (New York, 1920) are attained by the modern corporation. Property owners no longer exert much influence on the conduct of business; responsibility rests upon those by whom the work is conducted; and management has become a profession. But while the forms advocated by Tawney are more nearly here than a Fabian socialist could have thought likely in so short a time, Tawney would doubtless object that the spirit of the acquisitive society remains unchanged. (Cf. particularly his comments on pp. 96–97, and ch. 7 and *passim*.) For Brandeis' view, see L. D. Brandeis, *Business — A Profession* (Boston, 1914), pp. 1–12. Cf. also Mary Parker Follett, *Dynamic Administration* (New York and London, 1942).

interesting differences) with other bureaucracies, including governmental ones. For the general analysis of bureaucracy and for organization theory the study of the modern corporation is invaluable. Students of bureaucracy who follow the path marked out by Max Weber frequently stress the essential similarity in the main features of both governmental and "private" bureaucracies; students of public administration are much more prone to emphasize the peculiar features of governmental bureaucracies. The two emphases are not necessarily inconsistent. But they can not be integrated into a more comprehensive theory of bureaucratic organizations without systematic efforts to study and compare both kinds.

It is altogether possible, in fact, that the "public-private" dichotomy will prove to be less fruitful than a classification based upon a more complicated set of variables. For the study of bureaucracy is perhaps a special case of organization theory, to the recent growth of which H. A. Simon and J. G. March (both originally trained as political scientists) have greatly contributed. Simon's now classic *Administrative Behavior* cuts across the public-private distinction, as does the impressive new March-Simon work, *Organizations*.[14]

The internal government of the corporation, finally, has some bearing on the "power-structure" of the United States. A common populist and leftist view holds that politics is dominated by business, and business is dominated by an interlocking elite of financiers and directors. But Gordon's research casts doubt on the whole idea of effective control by interlocking directorates, and specifically by financial blocs. If corporate executives are controlled at all, it must be by price-cost considerations, monopolistic competition, professionalism, law, conscience, and so on. They are not, at any rate, controlled very extensively by their directors; at least this would be the conclusion to draw from Gordon's study.

Is the government of a corporation actually accessible to political scientists? There is some evidence that access may not be nearly so formidable as one imagines. March and R. Cyert, an economist, are

---

[14] H. A. Simon, *Administrative Behavior* (New York, 1947); J. G. March and H. A. Simon (with the collaboration of H. Guetzkow), *Organizations* (New York, 1958).

currently studying a handful of businesses in the Pittsburgh area in an attempt to construct models for decision-making that will forecast the behavior of business firms more reliably than those derived from the theory of the firm. Using data drawn from interviews and company records, March and Cyert attempt to "program" actual business decisions on a high-speed computer in order to compare the decision specified by their model with the decision made by the firm. The high-speed computer is, in effect, treated as decision-maker. The aim is not to substitute computers for business firms, but to develop and test models with high predictive value. The researchers make clear to the firms they study that no practical pay-off in improved procedures is in sight; but despite this, the firms have, so far, been remarkably cooperative in facilitating the investigation.[15]

Recent improvements in techniques for studying influence, resulting from the work of a number of political scientists engaged in studying community "power-structures," could be carried over almost intact to studies of the internal government of business firms. It will be ironic indeed if other social scientists transform themselves into political scientists, so to speak, in order to do the job that political scientists are not now doing.

Business Relations As A Political Order

Every organized system of relations has its economic aspects and its political aspects. That these have come to be treated in separate disciplines between which there is astonishingly little intellectual exchange is a fact frequently observed over a long period of time, and almost as frequently deplored. But the separation is still a fact. In defining what he means by the economic aspects of social organization,

---

[15] These studies are not yet published. However, cf. R. M. Cyert and J. G. March, "Organizational Structure and Pricing Behavior in an Oligopolistic Market," *American Economic Review,* Vol. 45 (March, 1955), pp. 129–39; *ibid.,* "Organizational Factors in the Theory of Oligopoly," *Quarterly Journal of Economics,* Vol. 70 (February, 1956), pp. 44–64; R. M. Cyert, H. A. Simon and D. B. Trow, "Observation of a Business Decision," *Journal of Business,* Vol. 29 (October, 1956), pp. 237–48.

the economist customarily ignores "influence" and "power" as explicit categories; but because economic theory seeks to describe an aspect of organized relationships existing in a well developed social order, implicit in every economic theory are some assumptions about influence relations. The model of a competitive price mechanism in a system of private property relations can easily be interpreted as an *explicit* description (in a language that can be translated into the language of politics) of the internal government of a particular economic order, or as a set of influence relations among actors within the economic order; and as an *implicit* description of certain relations existing among governmental officials and business men. But the explicit description is rarely translated into political language; and the implicit description generally remains implicit. Consequently a no-man's land has grown up between economics and political science. One can debate whether this no-man's land should be occupied by the discipline now called economics or the discipline now called political science; but it is difficult to argue persuasively that it should not be occupied at all by the social sciences.

The typical economist so conceives of his field of inquiry that when he employs his formal theoretical apparatus, he is not normally compelled to explicate many assumptions about the political aspects of the social system. The political theorist, by contrast, has historically found it difficult to ignore the economic aspects of the social system. For he has generally taken it for granted that different economic orders will have very significant effects for the distribution of influence over decisions in the "political" order.

Since the economist has a body of theory at hand, it might seem efficient for the political theorist to use the economist's models of different economic orders in order to provide himself with some relevant starting points. When he turns to economic theory, the political theorist does indeed discover an elaborately worked out model of a competitive price system embedded in what is surely one of the most, if not *the* most, complex, rigorous and intellectually demanding bodies of theory in the whole domain of the social sciences. But the model, for all its elegance, has only a restricted utility for a political scientist concerned with modern economic orders as complex and different as those of the USSR, the United States, and Indonesia. Even within the limited view assumed in this paper — American business and the American social system — the relations among giant firms like Dupont and General Motors raise immediate and obvious questions that are not dealt with by the existing models of economic theory.

Their relations do, on the other hand, have much in common with relations among states pursuing international strategies, invoking threats, penalties and rewards, engaging in negotiations and bargains, using propaganda and persuasion, seeking allies, and so on. There are also similarities with other forms of political rivalry and negotiation, such as conflict and compromise among leaders of political parties.

Economists have sometimes tried to break the grip of the competitive model. And in some of their descriptive writing on monopolies (where the theoretical biases of the economists have been curbed somewhat by the natural empiricism of lawyers), they seem to have succeeded. A large number of careful studies of the behavior of a particular firm, combination, industry, or segment of the economy display the spirit of critical empirical inquiry that guided the approach of earlier economists like J. M. Clark and Walton Hamilton. But in creating new theory to fit their descriptions, they do not seem to have been very successful, and possibly for good reasons. Veblen's iconoclastic *The Theory of Business Enterprise* (1904) seems to have had little impact on economic theory and perhaps even less on political science. Brady in his *Business As A System of Power* (New York, 1943) is concerned with precisely the kind of question political scientists would like to see treated; but he seems to have been so anxious to demonstrate that the United States was well on the way to Fascism that his treatment of the evidence is uncritical and at times even highly dubious. Theories of monopolistic competition have enabled economists to attack a new problem with relatively familiar weapons — but the fortress does not appear to have been taken. In any case, the *theoretical* writings on monopolistic competition and oligopoly (as distinct from the descriptive ones) are preoccupied with problems that are of only secondary interest to a political scientist.

Consequently a pressing need for new theory has developed. One new, relevant model would, at the moment, be worth a million facts; for until one or more relevant models is developed, it is difficult to know how additional facts can explain anything.

In such a situation, it is all too inviting to say that political science has much to offer. But it is precisely on questions of this kind that political theory is most primitive. The relations among large business firms, to be sure, might be subsumed under a general theory of bargaining. But political scientists have never produced a general theory of bargaining.

There are, however, some promising beginnings. The study of international politics includes the analysis of bargaining relations, and a few efforts have been made toward a general theory.[16] A new journal, *Conflict Resolution,* appeared in 1957; it has already published a considerable number of articles that at the very least must be considered as fragments of a possible general theory.[17] Relations among political leaders and parties are, of course, extensively described in the literature; and a number of writers have tried to explicate a theory to encompass these relations.[18] Economists have also been drawn into the search for an adequate theory. The older school of "institutional" economists led by John R. Commons was deeply interested in collective bargaining; Commons himself attempted to work out a general theory that would include bargaining relationships of many kinds.[19] Much later, J. K. Galbraith popularized the notion of "countervailing power," without, however, refining his theory very far.[20] N. Chamberlain has sought to explain by a bargaining theory many of the

[16] *Cf.* especially, M. Kaplan, *System and Process in International Politics* (New York, 1957).

[17] E.g., R. W. Mack and R. C. Snyder, "The Analysis of Social Conflict —Toward an Overview and Synthesis," Vol. I (June, 1957), pp. 212–47; H. Guetzkow, "Isolation and Collaboration: A Partial Theory of International Relations," Vol. I (March, 1957), pp. 48–68.

[18] E.g., Truman, *op. cit.;* E. Latham, *The Group Basis of Politics: A Study in Basing Point Legislation* (Ithaca, 1952); R. Dahl and C. Lindblom, *Politics, Economics and Welfare* (New York, 1953), chs. 12, 13, and 17.

[19] *The Economics of Collective Action* (New York, 1950).

[20] *American Capitalism: The Concept of Countervailing Power* (Boston, 1952).

relationships ordinarily treated in conventional economic theory.[21] In a monograph for the RAND Corporation, C. E. Lindblom set out an interpretation of bargaining as a generalized decision-process in politics and economics.[22] Some economists have been tempted by the theory of games developed by J. von Neuman and O. Morgenstern (himself an economist); probably the most elaborate exploitation of this lead by an economist is M. Shubik's study of competition and oligopoly, which uses the theory of games for its central theoretical apparatus.[23] Others have, however, rejected the game-theoretical approach as inadequate not only for relations among business firms but for most bargaining relationships, including, for example, those of international politics; thus Schelling appears to be in the process of creating a theoretical framework that may have some of the rigor of games theory and more relevance.[24] There is, then, a good deal of ferment; and it is reasonable to suppose that the problem of creating an adequate theory or set of theories about bargaining relationships will be attacked with much more vigor in the immediate future than it has been until very recently.

The extent to which contemporary social theory is intellectually stunted when it seeks to deal with the relations of giant business firms is a special case of a much vaster problem, one that I can only allude to here. It is not excessively wide of the mark to say that there is no theoretical apparatus powerful enough to provide even moderately useful answers to a very large number—quite possibly most—of the

---

[21] *A General Theory of Economic Process* (New York, 1955).

[22] *Bargaining: The Hidden Hand of Government* (RAND, Research memorandum RM-1434-RC, 1955); see also his "Policy Analysis," *American Economic Review*, Vol. 48 (June, 1958), pp. 298–312.

[23] *Competition, Oligopoly, and The Theory of Games* (Princeton, 1958). One should also consult H. Raiffa and D. Luce, *Games and Decisions* (New York, 1957), ch. 6, "Two-Person Cooperative Games"; J. F. Nash, "The Bargaining Problem," *Econometrica*, Vol. 18 (April, 1950), pp. 155–62; J. Pen, "A General Theory of Bargaining," *American Economic Review*, Vol. 42 (March, 1952). For a summary and synthesis, see Allan Cartter, *Theory of Wages and Employment* (New York, 1959), pp. 24–42.

[24] T. C. Schelling, "An Essay on Bargaining," *American Economic Review*, Vol. 46 (June, 1956), pp. 281–306; "Bargaining, Communication, and Limited War," *Conflict Resolution*, Vol. 1 (March, 1957), pp. 19–36.

questions generated by the diversity and complexity of contemporary economic orders. And it is exceedingly doubtful whether theory adequate to the task can be developed by economists, except in so far as they concern themselves with the political aspects of social relations,[25] or by political scientists except in so far as they concern themselves with economic aspects. Indeed, it is altogether plausible that the existing division of labor within the social sciences as a whole is working strongly against the development of the kind of theory that is most needed.

Business and the American Political Order

THE GENERAL STATE OF THE DISCIPLINE

The task of tracing out past manifestations of the relations between businessmen and the political order has been left mostly to historians.[26] It is at least arguable that with the kinds of data available the questions a political scientist might like to put can not be answered anyway. But surely this is a premature conclusion. In general when skillful social scientists turn their scholarly attention to historical problems, they manage to ask new questions and get new answers.[27]

But even on the relations between business and the existing political order, the subject is in a curiously incomplete state. In the late 1920s and early 1930s some pioneering work was undertaken; and if this work has, by now, been pretty thoroughly assimilated into the main body of American political science, its specific concerns have not, by

[25] This view is shared by a number of economists; e.g., Arthur Ross, in *Trade Union Wage Policy* (Berkeley, 1956), concludes that unions must be considered essentially as political organizations.

[26] E.g., Miriam Beard, *A History of the Businessman* (New York, 1938); A. M. Schlesinger, Sr., *Colonial Merchants of the Revolution* (New York, 1917); R. A. East, *Business Enterprise in the American Revolutionary Era* (New York, 1938); T. C. Cockran and W. Miller, *The Age of Enterprise* (New York, 1942).

[27] As evidence, I would offer L. Hartz, *Economic Policy and Democratic Thought: Pennsylvania, 1776–1860* (Cambridge, 1948); L. D. White, *The Federalists 1789–1801* (New York, 1948), and the three succeeding volumes in his administrative history; M. J. Dauer, *The Adams Federalists* (Baltimore, 1953).

and large, been pursued. In that period the older legalistic and institutional view of political activity was breaking up under the impact
of the new realism offered by men like Charles Merriam; Bentley and
his group interpretation of politics were having a belated effect on the
thinking of the *avant garde;* and pluralistic ideas had moved across the
Atlantic to find a ready reception in the United States. In 1921, F. W.
Coker's, "The Technique of the Pluralistic State" appeared in *The
American Political Science Review*.[28] In 1929, E. P. Herring's pioneering
work, *Group Representation Before Congress,* embodied many of the
new ways of interpreting politics.[29] In the following year, H. L.
Childs' study of the American Federation of Labor and the U. S.
Chamber of Commerce appeared; it carried a preface by Merriam
and an acknowledgment by Childs of his debt to Merriam and also
to Coker. Although somewhat pedestrian in execution, the book was
thoroughly in the new spirit; it concluded with the observation:
"Periodic elections are turning into periodic competitions between
personalities, while the day-to-day process of governing a great nation
turns into a continuous balancing of pressing interests of more and
more highly perfected organized group interests." (p. 260). Later E.
E. Schattschneider undertook his now classic study of the pressures on
Congress during the Smoot-Hawley tariff controversy of 1929–1930;
the book appeared in 1935.[30]

---

[28] Vol. 15 (May, 1921), pp. 186–214. Cf. also M. P. Follett, *The New State* (New
York, 1918) and E. D. Ellis, "The Pluralistic State," *The American Political Science
Review,* Vol. 14 (August, 1920), pp. 393–407.

[29] Baltimore, 1929. His *Public Administration and the Public Interest,* which reflects a
similar approach, appeared seven years later (New York, 1936). Concern with pressure groups and lobbying has remained at a fairly high level. For example, B. Zeller,
Pressure Politics in New York (New York, 1937); D. D. McKean, *Pressures on the Legislature of New Jersey* (New York, 1938); D. C. Blaisdell, *Economic Power and Political
Pressures* (T.N.E.C. Monograph No. 26, Washington, 1941); *Unofficial Government:
Pressure Groups and Lobbies,* D. C. Blaisdell, ed., *The Annals,* Vol. 319 (September,
1958). That the concern with "interest groups" and "pressures" is no longer an Ameri-
can hobby is indicated by the recent publication of *Interest Groups on Four Continents,*
H. W. Ehrmann, ed. (Pittsburgh, 1958).

[30] *Politics, Pressures and the Tariff* (New York, 1935). A more recent analysis of
business attitudes on the tariff reveals a striking reversal of opinion since the days of
Smoot-Hawley; cf. R. A. Bauer, S. Keller, and I. de S. Pool, *What American Trade*

From that time forward there has been no equivalent period of innovation and regeneration. V. O. Key's textbook on political parties appeared in 1942 with a section on business as a pressure group that has been modified and carried through each succeeding edition. It is a remarkably succinct and comprehensive discussion of the major aspects of business-in-politics; one might reasonably have expected it to stimulate considerable research interest among its many readers.[31]

Latham's detailed examination of the fate of basing-point legislation in Congress appeared in book form in 1952,[32] followed two years later by a shorter case study by Garceau and Silverman dealing with the activities of the Associated Industries of Vermont in the 1951 session of the Vermont legislature.[33] The casebook edited by Harold Stein, *Public Administration and Policy Formation* (New York, 1952) and the ICP series that followed have some significant cases involving the relations of business and government. Doubtless one could cite other items; but what is surprising is the extent to which the earlier interest seems to have tapered off.[34]

What seems to have happened is that the Great Depression and the New Deal turned the attention of political scientists away from explaining behavior to prescribing policy. Significantly, the first of the Harvard series entitled *Public Policy* appeared in 1940; it reflects the newer concern with reform and regulation. The study of government regulation, to which I have already alluded, now began to thrive.

Policy Does American Business Want? (Center for International Studies, M.I.T., Cambridge, 1955). Bauer and de S. Pool also have a forthcoming book, *American Businessmen and International Trade: Code Book and Data from a Study on Attitudes and Communications* (Glencoe, 1959).

[31] *Politics, Parties, and Pressure Groups* (New York, 1958, 4th ed.), ch. 4.

[32] E. Latham, *The Group Basis of Politics, A Study in Basing Point Legislation* (Ithaca, 1952). Latham has a forthcoming volume, *The Politics of Railroad Coordination, 1933–1936* (Cambridge, 1959), and an essay, "The Body Politic of the Corporation" (to be published by the Fund for the Republic under the editorship of Edward S. Mason).

[33] O. Garceau and C. Silverman, "A Pressure Group and the Pressured: a Case Report," *The American Political Science Review*, Vol. 48 (September, 1954), pp. 672–91.

[34] Among the exceptions: J. W. Prothro, *The Dollar Decade, Business Ideas in the 1920's* (Baton Rouge, 1954); J. Palamountain, *The Politics of Distribution* (Cambridge, 1955); R. W. Gable, "NAM: Influential Lobby or Kiss of Death?" *The Journal of Politics*, Vol. 15 (May, 1953).

However, many of the political scientists who occupied themselves with regulation were primarily concerned with administrative activities rather than "politics" (if I may be permitted a distinction that is widely regarded as *passé,* and may therefore be due for revival); and the kind of inquiry begun by Herring and Schattschneider was not carried forward. It may be, too, that the sort of clinical detachment that would enable the observer to put his moral commitments about "business" to one side long enough to observe the underlying forces at work was impossible in the temper of the Thirties and the crisis of War.

It may be possible now to pick up where the earlier writers left off, or even to start with newer insights and ideas. Lane's *The Regulation of Businessmen,* which appeared in 1954, presented a psycho-cultural interpretation of the problems of regulation that displays the kind of ferment of new ideas that marked the work of the earlier period.[35]

THE FACTORS TO BE CONSIDERED

We are in the position, then, of having made a good start, even an exciting start. But we are hardly set for the long pull. Let me now consider very briefly some factors relevant to the problem of assessing the political roles of business in the contemporary order. I shall then undertake to examine what has been done, and what needs to be done, under these heads.

To the extent that one is concerned with relations of influence, the following questions need to be answered:

1 What distinctions shall one make among the individuals or groups under investigation? "Business" is, after all, as various a phenomenon as "politics"; and taken simply in the large it may prove to have almost no meaning at all.

2 What is the *basis* of the influence of one actor on another? That is, what kinds of resources are available to him for influencing the other?

[35] New Haven, 1954.

3 How does he actually use these resources, if at all? What are his *techniques*?

4 In what parts of the political order does he employ these techniques? What is the political space or *arena* within which the influence relationship exists?

5 On what kinds of matters, subjects, or responses? What is the *scope* of the relationship?

6 How great an effect do the techniques actually have? How successful is the effort to exert influence? Or, in other words, what is the *magnitude* of the influence?

In addition to these six elements, which help to make precise any statements one might care to make about the influence of businessmen on politicians and bureaucrats, or of politicians and bureaucrats on businessmen, one might wish to answer some other questions in order to assess the political roles of businessmen. For example:

7 What kinds of *motives* help to explain the political roles of businessmen? E.g., what are the motivations of businessmen in their political relationships?

8 What *attitudes* — their own or those of others — are involved in political relationships?

9 What *ideologies,* comprehensive outlooks, or underlying structures of attitudes are at work?

The remainder of this section of my paper will consist, then, of a brief examination of the present state of our knowledge with respect to each of these questions, and the problems and possibilities of further inquiry.

DISTINCTIONS AMONG BUSINESSMEN

Differences in the political behavior of businessmen may be almost as significant as similarities. "Aims of different elements of the business community often diverge," Key writes. "Yet it cannot be denied that on some types of questions considerable cohesiveness prevails within the business community . . . . On all these matters investigation and discerning reflection are limited enough to leave us with wide areas of ignorance."[36]

It is a plausible and commonplace hypothesis that in some respects the political behavior of businessmen is a function of the size of the firm. The social, psychological, and economic environment of the small businessman is often thought to be more conducive to extremism and intolerance than the bureaucratized and technical setting of the big businessman. But there is slight evidence on the point. In sample surveys the numbers of businessmen interviewed are usually too small to permit distinctions; consequently differences in attitudes that might be associated with size of business firms are left unexplained or are attributed to other factors, such as education.[37] Thus Stouffer's study of attitudes toward Communists and other dissenters reveals wide differences between well educated and poorly educated businessmen; but there are no breakdowns according to size of firm — and it is more than likely that size of firm and extent of education are highly associated.[38] However, in a study of support for McCarthy and political tolerance in Bennington, Vt., Trow found the expected relation. Surprisingly enough, when education is held constant, he found very little difference between the attitude of manual workers and middle class people on freedom of speech and McCarthy's methods. But within the middle class itself, the salaried employees and small entrepreneurs were not only different in social origins and educational attainments but in their political orientations as well. Only a third of the small businessmen and merchants had gone to college, compared with half of the salaried employees. Taking only the high school graduates, or only those who had gone to college, the proportion who supported McCarthy was very much larger for small businessmen than for salaried employees. He found, moreover, that the small

---

[36] V. O. Key, *op. cit.*, 3d ed. (New York, 1952), p. 118.

[37] The study by Bauer, Keller, and Pool (see footnote 30) is an important exception.

[38] Cf. "The Businessman and Civil Liberties," *Fortune,* May, 1955, pp. 114–15. These data in *Fortune* were a part of a larger study, but were omitted from the book, *Communism, Conformity, and Civil Liberties* (New York, 1955).

businessmen were also more hostile toward big business and labor unions than the salaried employees (again with education held constant).[39]

One would also expect political behavior to vary with certain other characteristics of the firm, such as its geographical location, sources of supplies, markets, vulnerability to competition, and so on. Examples are easily found to underscore the point. Thus, at one time the opposition of the importer to tariffs was "taken for granted [in Congress], discounted in advance, and . . . heard . . . with irritation."[40] The situation has probably changed a good deal in three decades.[41] Or, to take another case, the growing foreign market for American automobiles is thought to account for the recent support given to reciprocal trade agreements by some leading automotive manufacturers. (What the growth in the American market for foreign cars will do remains to be seen.) Or again, because of the peculiar importance of state and federal regulatory bodies in the lives of public utilities, some of them have invested heavily in the art of influencing public opinion; the president of the Bell System was aware of the need for public support as early as 1913.[42]

It is important, too, to distinguish businessmen who are relatively active in politics from those who are not. It is possible that demographic variables together with the character of business firms will account for much of the variation in the political behavior of businessmen. But almost certainly these factors will not account for anything like *all* of the variation; they may not even account for enough of it to assure us that we are on the right track. Some businessmen (not many) are relatively active in politics; a great many others are not. How can we account for the difference? A neo-Marxist explanation would have it that some businessmen serve as the specialized representatives of the

[39] Martin Trow, *Support for McCarthy and Political Tolerance in a New England Town* (mimeographed, 1956), ch. II, "Class and Occupation."

[40] Schattschneider, *op. cit.,* pp. 159 ff.

[41] See L. A. Dexter, "Congressmen and the People they Listen To" (mimeographed, 1955).

[42] Norton Long, "Public Relations of the Bell System," *Public Opinion Quarterly* (October, 1937), p. 18.

entire business community; and there is a rough and ready sense in which this may indeed be the case. But the explanation does not fit well with the heterogeneity of the business community; in any case, the proposition is no more than an extremely general hypothesis with only superficial plausibility. As Schattschneider concluded from his study of the tariff fight of 1929–1930, "Contrary to facile assumptions, economic interests . . . are not universally active in promoting their interests in politics. . . . The political activity of economic groups seems . . . to be no more uniform than it is universal. Apparently, equal stakes do not produce equal pressures."[43]

THE VARIOUS BASES AND TECHNIQUES OF INFLUENCE

It is conventional to assume that if businessmen — some business-men — have influence over political decisions rather greater than that of the mythical average citizen, the basis of their enhanced influence is their larger wealth and income, in short, their "money." For techniques of influence are usually expensive. The more money one can dispose of — to put the matter in very general fashion — the more one has available to spend on techniques of influence.

It might be wise at this juncture to make a distinction between techniques of direct influence over policy-makers, such as campaign contributions and lobbying, and techniques of indirect influence. Thanks to the assiduous work of some Congressional committees, Louise Overacker, and Alexander Heard, the subject of campaign contributions has been rather thoroughly worked over (although only a part of Heard's work has yet been published). There is also a considerable body of material on lobbying, much of which deals with lobbying by business organizations. Most of this work on campaign contributions and lobbying is, of course, well known to political scientists.[44]

43 *Op. cit.,* p. 163.

44 On campaign contributions see Louise Overacker, *Presidential Campaign Funds* (Boston, 1946), *Money in Elections* (New York, 1932), and numerous articles in *The American Political Science Review;* J. K. Pollock, *Party Campaign Funds* (New York, 1926); U. S. Senate, 84th Cong., 2d sess., Hearings on 1956 Presidential and Senatorial Campaign Practices (1956) and 1956 General Election Campaigns (1957); A. Heard, *Money and Politics* (Washington, 1956); his forthcoming work is entitled *The Costs of Democracy.* On lobbying, cf. Key, *op. cit.* (4th ed.) ch. 6 and *passim.*

Yet while we know a satisfying amount about the techniques, we know very little about how successful they are. The problem of estimating magnitudes of influence is a formidable one; it is probably not too harsh to say that all we have at present are very detailed and conscientious studies of techniques and very little worthwhile evidence bearing on their success.

In addition to the techniques that depend mainly on "money" are those that depend on "organization." In making his case for the "power elite" of big business executives, government executives, and military leaders, Mills speaks of "institutional means of power" and "the command posts": the key positions at the head of key organizations. We are informed that the members of his tripartite elite occupy "the command posts of the big hierarchies" ("nation-wide hierarchies of power and wealth").[45] But unless I have quite thoroughly misread him, Mills does not attempt to show at all precisely *how* these organizational hierarchies convey power, nor how *much* power they convey. One is left with the impression that Mills has displayed a good deal of useful information about some elite groups; but whether they are elites of *power* is quite another question. Whatever one may conclude about Mills' general thesis, however, there can be no doubt that he has pointed to a possible basis of influence in organizational structures which needs to be thoroughly investigated and analyzed.

One source of influence that may be undergoing some significant changes is control over employment within a firm. Until a few decades ago, control over employment probably gave the business leader considerably more influence over the overt political behavior of the worker than it does now. Paradoxically, as firms have grown bigger they have found it more difficult to exploit the employment relationship as a lever to control the political conduct of their workers. The old fashioned company town has become much less common. In the

---

[45] C. W. Mills, *The Power Elite* (New York, 1956), pp. 23–71 and *passim*. The idea may have been suggested by Karl Mannheim, who in his *Man and Society in an Age of Reconstruction* (London, 1940) spoke of "key positions" in a rather similar sense (pp. 153–54, 194, 202, 231, 363). It is significant that under the influence of the benign political institutions of Great Britain, Mannheim pretty much left these earlier views behind in his *Freedom, Power and Democratic Planning* (New York, 1950).

giant firms, the worker is usually protected by trade unions; and even where unions are absent, bureaucratization, impersonality, and modern personnel practices have generally replaced direct intervention into the workers' life. Many large firms propagandize their workers through company brochures and house organs, but the effects are difficult to estimate. Occasionally a firm will successfully stimulate its employees to "bring pressure" on public officials where some matter of common economic interest is involved; probably the threat of foreign competition to a protected industry offers the firmest grounds for political unity between management and workers. The techniques of "pressure" are almost invariably the conventional ones: writing letters or sending telegrams, usually with a common phrasing and style that betrays their inspiration; occasionally, however, a firm will encourage its employees to call on their Congressmen whenever the opportunity arises.

But there are three important respects in which one must qualify the hypothesis that employees have grown politically more independent of their employing firms in recent years. In the first place, the rapid expansion of "security" tests for employees in firms that have even the slightest connection with national defense has put an exceptionally powerful means into the hands of employers; and it is a means that until the present remains virtually unregulated by public authorities.[46] In the second place, the mushrooming of welfare funds and pension trust funds has created vast new opportunities for control. Of the welfare funds administered by trade unions, we have recently heard a great deal by virtue of Congressional exposés. But much less is known about the power over employees provided by pension funds. Berle writes:

There is a gradually growing feeling that pension trusts, for example, must be controlled. A pension trust ring could be something to bind a man beyond belief. It could bind him to his job. He could not change it without losing a substantial part of his life savings. He might be controlled in all sorts of ways. We are beginning to think even that the pension trust right which cannot be transferred to some other pension trust is suspect.[47]

[46] Ralph Brown, *Loyalty and Security* (New Haven, 1958), chs. 5–7, 18.
[47] A. A. Berle, Jr., *Economic Power and the Free Society*.

In the third place, if (despite these two additional factors) workers have grown more independent, it seems altogether likely that executives and white collar workers have grown more docile. From workers, "the company" formerly secured an unwilling and overt compliance that could not endure once the balance of power shifted slightly. From executives and office employees, the compliance is evidently willing and even enthusiastic. Whyte's thesis on the rise of the organization man is too well known to need repetition here, but it is obvious that the existence of a broad layer of politically docile corporate executives and white collar workers could have profound consequences for the operation of the political system.[48]

On none of these questions is there much evidence one way or another. Nor are we better off when we turn to specific political activities of businessmen. Like upper socioeconomic groups generally, their level of political activity as expressed in voting, campaign contributions, and political work is considerably above average; but the great bulk evidently content themselves with voting and discussing politics.[49] In his study of the social backgrounds of political decision-makers, Mathews found that "proprietors and officials" constituted between a fifth and a fourth of state legislators, state governors, Congressmen, Senators, and Presidents, vice-presidents, and cabinet members for various recent periods; the category was represented at a rate about three times its frequency in the labor force.[50] But again the category "proprietors and officials" is very broad; more detailed

[48] W. H. Whyte, *The Organization Man* (New York, 1956); C. Wright Mills, *White Collar* (New York, 1953); A. Hacker, *op. cit.*

[49] In the often quoted survey by Woodward and Roper, about a third of the "executives" interviewed were rated as "very active" politically. According to the scoring system used, an individual who voted regularly, discussed politics frequently, and belonged to a political party was rated as "very active." Cf. J. L. Woodward and E. Roper, "Political Activity of American Citizens," *The American Political Science Review*, Vol. 44 (December, 1950), pp. 872–85. In response to the question "Have you ever written or wired your Congressman or Senator in Washington?," 67 per cent of the "professional and business" respondents of the American Institute of Public Opinion answered "No." (AIPO, September 24, 1949).

[50] D. R. Mathews, *The Social Background of Political Decision-makers* (New York, 1954), Table 7, p. 30. Cf. also his "United States Senators and the Class Structure," in *Political Behavior* (Glencoe, 1956), pp. 184–92.

studies would be needed before one could differentiate among types of businessmen.

If we turn the question of bases and techniques around in order to look at it from the side of government — what bases and techniques are available to government leaders for influencing the behavior of businessmen? — we move from an uncharted sea into the whole ocean of political science. There are, none the less, some points worth keeping in mind. The question is of professional interest not only to political scientists but also to economists and lawyers; in some universities one can find courses on government control of business not only in the two social science departments but in the faculty of law as well. An examination of textbooks indicates that economists tend to treat the subject in rather narrow terms; they are, for example, fascinated by the anti-trust problem — which is, after all, a narrow segment of the whole domain. Political scientists are more inclined to a broader view, although they are prone to emphasize the legal and administrative aspects to the exclusion of "politics." Moreover, even among political scientists the treatment is heavily descriptive and non-theoretical.

The reason for this is probably not obscure: there is no existing body of theory adequate to the task of dealing with the intermediate areas between politics and economics. When the economist tries to extend his theory to cover governmental and political behavior, the results are unimpressive. Probably the most interesting and imaginative recent effort is Anthony Downs' *An Economic Theory of Democracy*,[51] which is a bold, vigorous, and lucid application of some of the economist's modes of thought to the task of constructing a comprehensive theory of the behavior of democratic systems. The book is less useful to a political scientist looking for a theory to explain "economic" behavior in "political" terms than it is to an economist seeking to make sense out of "political" behavior in "economic" terms. But it is unquestionably an important step forward in a field of inquiry where institutional and descriptive approaches by political scientists, and arid model building by economists, have all but stifled the growth of relevant theory.

[51] New York, 1957.

If we turn now from more or less direct techniques to the indirect means by which businessmen may influence the actions of governments (and conversely) we face one of the most important and at the same time one of the most difficult assignments open to a contemporary social scientist. Perhaps the importance of such an analysis, and the difficulty too, can be suggested by comparing several alternative and drastically over-simple models of the political process in a "democratic" society. In the conventional normative model, the political leader is usually viewed as an agent of majority opinion. In the conventional "pressure" model, he is an agent of unequally weighted "pressures" brought to bear by individuals and groups with varying bases of influence, techniques, and degrees of success. If we regard the "pressures" that bear directly on the political leader as first-order forces, the pressure model can be made both more complicated and more interesting if it is enlarged to include forces of the second order, third order, and *n*th order: i.e., the activities that generate these activities, and so on. In one oversimplified and extreme variant, the political leaders are assumed to be substantially autonomous — they themselves generate all the pressures to which they respond. In another extreme variant, the elected leaders are completely subject to "pressures" generated by autonomous elements elsewhere in the system. "Business" might be treated as an (or the) autonomous element.

Once we begin tracing out the chain of political forces to their "ultimate" sources, we move into a problem that liberal-democratic theory has found it more and more difficult to deal with. As Frank Knight has often pointed out, liberal theory tended to take individual preferences for granted; preferences were in some sense the ultimate irreducible atoms with which the liberal constructed his theory. But the atoms have proved to be reducible, after all, to more primitive elements.

The question is germane to our concern here primarily because of the rise of "modern" techniques for influencing opinion, and their adoption by business to influence individuals not only as consumers but also as citizens. Leaders who represent wealth and property have long recognized the importance of public opinion for the maintenance of their condition. The election of 1840 might be taken as a convenient landmark, for in that election the Whigs finally turned their backs on the hopelessly outdated Federalist tradition of a dominant elite maintaining its rule independent of mass opinion. But as Kelley shows, it was not until about 1900 that large American business firms dropped their policy of aloofness toward public opinion and began to cultivate it. In 1902, Ida Tarbell discovered the changed approach in Standard Oil. In 1904, Ivy Lee and George Parker created their press bureau to explain and defend business before the public. By 1952, *Fortune* has estimated, there were 5,000 companies in the United States supporting public relations departments at an annual cost for supervisory *personnel* alone of around $400 million.[52] Mr. B. J. Mullaney, "director of the utility interests' Illinois information committee during their multi-million-dollar propaganda campaign of the nineteen-twenties," uttered the classic formulation of the importance of indirect techniques when he said:

When a destructive bill is pending in a legislature it has to be dealt with in a way to get results. I am not debating that. But to depend, year after year, upon the usual political expedients for stopping hostile legislation is shortsightedness. In the long run isn't it better and surer to lay a groundwork with the people back home who have the votes, so that proposals of this character are not popular with them, rather than depend upon stopping such proposals when they get up to the legislature or commission?[53]

In 1937, Norton Long wrote his doctoral dissertation at Harvard on the public relations policies of the Bell Telephone Company; part of the dissertation appeared that year in *Public Opinion Quarterly*.[54] So far as I can discover, no political scientist took up the topic again until Kelley's book (originally a dissertation at Johns Hopkins) appeared in 1956. In his analysis, Kelley offers four case studies of "particular public relations men at work in particular campaigns"; these include the

    [52] Stanley Kelley, Jr., *Professional Public Relations and Political Power* (Baltimore, 1956), pp. 9–12.
    [53] Senate Document 92, Part 71A, 70th Cong., 1st sess., p. 17, quoted in Kelley, pp. 12–13.
    [54] "The Public Relations Policies of the Bell System" (PH.D. dissertation, Harvard, 1937) and "Public Relations of the Bell System."

general activities of the firm of Whitaker and Baxter in California, their specific work for the AMA campaign against national health insurance, the Maryland senatorial campaign of 1950, and the 1952 presidential campaign.

As Kelley describes the assumptions of Whitaker and Baxter, one has the impression that they have unconsciously codified into operating principles many of the hypotheses about voting behavior that a careful reader of recent election studies might also make — assumptions that on the whole run flatly counter to the behavior prescribed in the normative models of democracy. The points of convergence and divergence would be worth examining. It would also be important to have more evidence bearing on the success of these efforts; but this is an enormously difficult problem, and one I propose to come back to in a moment.

The Different Levels of Government

There are numerous "arenas" within which these techniques can be applied. Here I propose only to examine the accepted ones: the local community, the state, the national government, and the international areas. Of these, the relations between business and national government have been by a very large margin the most thoroughly studied. There are probably several reasons for this: the greater saliency of the regulatory activities of the national government, the amount of material made available by public bodies, the general bias of American political scientists toward the national government, and the relatively less difficult methodological and investigatory problems involved in studying politics at that level.

On this subject as on most others the state governments are perhaps the most neglected. In addition to the article by Garceau and Silverman mentioned above, the only book by a political scientist dealing with the relations between business and the states appears to be Fesler's study of the independence of state regulatory agencies.[55]

In recent years, political scientists have left the systematic study of

---

[55] J. W. Fesler, *The Independence of State Regulatory Agencies* (1942).

the local community largely to sociologists, whose preoccupation with social status and class has produced a curious, if mostly implicit, bias in their findings on politics. For these studies have tended to assume, not always explicitly, that social status and political influence are very highly correlated. The Lynds (and, long before, Lincoln Steffens), Warner, Hollingshead, Withers, and Hunter all discover a socioeconomic elite that is also "influential" in the community.[56] Nearly all the interesting questions are, however, swamped by a positive correlation between some sort of social status and some sort of influence. The important question might be formulated this way: On what kinds of issues are what kinds of people influential with whom? The evidence of these studies, unfortunately, does not permit an answer to this question.

A number of current investigations in various stages of completion will almost certainly enable us to handle the problem with more precision than before.[57] Meanwhile, we are not totally in the dark. Mills departs from his colleagues in arguing that the new elites are nationwide in character; to those new elites, he contends, influence over local politics is of negligible importance.[58] There is a considerable amount of suggestive evidence for his hypothesis. The executives of national firms are often too much on the move to settle more than superficially into local politics.[59] Moreover, the outcome of local

[56] R. S. and H. M. Lynd, *Middletown* (New York, 1931) and *Middletown in Transition* (New York, 1937); W. L. Warner, *The Social Life of a Modern Community* (New Haven, 1941); A. Hollingshead, *Elmtown's Youth* (New York, 1949); J. West (C. Withers), *Plainville, U.S.A.* (New York, 1945); F. Hunter, *Community Power Structure* (Chapel Hill, 1953).

[57] These studies include San Francisco (by G. Belknap), Atlanta (by F. Cleaveland), Boston (by N. Long), Chicago (by E. Banfield), and New Haven (by R. Dahl).

[58] C. W. Mills, *The Power Elite*, ch. 2, "Local Society."

[59] Some industrialists do appeal to their brethren to be more active in politics. At the annual meeting of the American Petroleum Institute in Chicago, Ill., in November, 1958, L. R. Boulware, vice-president of General Electric (and a former War Production Board official), asked each industrialist to visit and convert fifty families to "a sound way of thinking and to an immunity to demagogues." At the same meeting, however, G. Romney, president of the American Motors Corporation "counselled big companies to stay out of politics. Instead of duplicating labor's political activities, business should 'deplore' them." *The New York Times*, November 12, 1958.

disputes usually can have only marginal effects on the large firm. Although many firms cultivate "community relations," there is a strong suggestion that what they are mostly interested in is good will — which they can lose by too much activity in local politics. If one can judge from some of the handbooks on community relations, the most highly regarded strategy among professionals is to commit oneself to politically neutral causes like the local community chest drive (which typically is headed mostly by men from the business community) and to avoid "politics" like the plague. One book lists 29 "don'ts," which are summarized: "Don't do anything, if it can be avoided, that will damage the community, injure or irritate its people, offend its traditions or customs, or otherwise show disregard for the well-being or good will of the community." The positive injunctions are equally innocuous.[60]

However, communities and business firms vary tremendously. Dupont executives appear to dominate Aiken, S. C., in a way that General Electric executives do not, and perhaps could not, in Schenectady. It is reasonable to suppose that the extent to which a firm attempts to influence political decisions in a community is a function of a number of variables, including the traditions of the firm, the size of the community, the extent of the community's economic dependence on the firm, and the existence and aggressiveness of trade unions. A great many more local studies will be necessary before the full range of existing relations between businessmen and local governments has been adequately explored.

At the international level the researcher has until recently had very little to turn to in the way of concrete case studies. A few years ago, the National Planning Association began a series of case studies of the performance of United States business abroad: Sears, Roebuck in Mexico, Grace in Peru, Firestone in Liberia, etc. Although the studies

[60] Cf. L. B. Lundborg, *Public Relations in the Local Community* (New York, 1950), pp. 68, 76, 78, 94, 206, 210; and F. R. Henderer, *A Comparative Study of the Public Relations Practises in Six Industrial Corporations* (Pittsburgh, 1956), p. 109. However, see S. H. Walker and P. Sklar, *Business Finds its Voice: Management's Effort to Sell the Business Idea to the Public* (New York, 1938).

vary in content and quality they are thorough and comprehensive.[61] In view of the fact that in many parts of the world the business firm deals with local populations—and local politicians—with a directness and impact greater than that of our formal representatives, it is obvious that the relation of the international firm to American foreign policies is a matter of highest importance. To take a little known example, Sears opened its first store in Latin America in Havana in 1942 and now has 60 retail outlets in Mexico, Brazil, Venezuela, Colombia, and Peru, employing close to 10,000 people, of whom less than 2 per cent are North Americans.[62] The importance of the oil companies in South America and in the Middle East is so well-known and so obvious that it needs no emphasis. Yet the relationships between the international corporation and American policy remain largely in the domain of gossip and speculation.

SCOPE AND MAGNITUDE

Although the *scope* and *magnitude* of influence are analytically separable, it will be convenient in this survey to deal with them together. But it is essential to keep in mind that they are not the same thing. Over one scope—e.g., legislation in Congress on taxes—an actor may have a large amount of influence; at the same time, over another scope—e.g., legislation in Congress on foreign policy—he may have only negligible influence. Consequently no statement about the amount of influence an actor exerts has much meaning unless it contains a reference to the scope. Failing to adhere to this simple requirement has probably accounted for more obfuscation about the "power" of various groups than any other single factor.

In principle, it is possible to rank actors according to the magnitude of their influence over a given scope. One can do this by asking with respect to each actor: How great a change in the probability of an

---

[61] Under the general title *United States Business Performance Abroad*, the monographs include *Sears, Roebuck De Mexico, S.A.* (1953), *Casa Grace in Peru* (1954), *The Philippine American Life Insurance Company* (1955), *The Creole Petroleum Corporation in Venezuela* (1955), *The Firestone Operations in Liberia* (1956).

[62] T. V. Houser, *Big Business and Human Values* (New York, 1957) pp. 69–78.

event taking place can be attributed solely to the activities of this actor? If nature and social action generously provide one with the appropriate information, one can then say that A is (or is not) more influential than B with respect to a given scope. But we can not rank scopes, at least not without some "outside" criterion that has to be supplied by the researcher. Thus (in principle) it would be possible to say (meaningfully) that on matters of tax assessments in Jonesville, Smith is more influential than Brown; and on matters of school policy, Brown is more influential than Smith. But unless we agree in advance that school policy is in some sense "more important" than assessments, and therefore must have a greater weight, one can not say that over the whole range of assessments *and* school policy, Brown is more influential than Smith; it will be readily seen that assigning weights would, at best, present a formidable problem.

The bearing of all this on our present discussion is that the more closely one sticks to statements about the influence of *x* class of businessmen over *y* category of outcomes (at time *t*), the more obvious and unambiguous is one's meaning, and the easier it is to test the truth of what one says. But the more one tries to speak about the "general" influence of business in American politics, the more ambiguous one's meaning and the more difficult to test for truth. Therefore any over-all assessment of the influence of businessmen on politicians, or *vice versa,* must be regarded as a kind of loose summary statement, the meaning of which must be sought for in a set of concrete propositions.

It is possible, nonetheless, to distinguish some approaches to the problem of over-all assessment of the influence of business in American life that differ radically in their assumptions (which are usually explicit only in part) as to scopes and magnitudes of influence.

The simplest and most straightforward way of looking at the matter is to hypothesize that there is a single dominant locus for arriving at political decisions, and a single, homogeneous group in control of the dominant locus. In this respect the Marxist and his ultra-conservative critic (who sees businessmen as completely dominated by politicians and bureaucrats) stand, intellectually, shoulder to shoulder. There are a number of important modifications of this approach. To Veblen,

"Representative government means, chiefly, representation of business interests. The government commonly works in the interest of business men with a fairly consistent singleness of purpose."[63] Writing in 1904, Veblen was not perhaps so wide of the mark. In various ways and with various modifications, the Lynds, Brady, Mills, Hunter, and even Burnham at one stage adopt a similar viewpoint.[64]

At the other extreme are neo-pluralists like Truman, Key, and Latham (and perhaps Berle) who suggest that there are a number of loci for arriving at political decisions; that businessmen, trade unions, politicians, consumers, farmers, voters, and many other aggregates all have an impact on policy outcomes; that none of these aggregates is homogeneous for all purposes; that each of them is highly influential over some scopes but weak over many others; and that the power to reject undesired alternatives is more common than the power to dominate over outcomes directly.[65]

The difficulty in choosing among these views, or even in developing another variant, is that we do not have anything like enough carefully formulated case studies of the roles of businessmen in politics. To be sure, library shelves sag with cases in law, business and public administration. But few if any of these cases are useful for testing hypotheses about influence, for the relevant questions were not in the minds of the authors.

It is perhaps a general characteristic of political science that we know a good deal more about techniques than we do about effects, partly, no doubt, because it is comparatively easy to observe and describe techniques and enormously difficult to measure effects. The difficulty of measuring effects is compounded by the fact that beliefs about the extent of business influence over government (and *vice versa*) serve psychological, ideological, and even economic functions. Lobbyists, advertisers, and public relations experts have a self-serving interest in

[63] *The Theory of Business Enterprise* (New York, 1904, 1935), p. 286.

[64] O. R. Brady, *Business as a System of Power* (New York, 1943); J. Burnham, *The Managerial Revolution* (New York, 1941). See also citations in footnote 56.

[65] It is an interesting and perhaps significant fact that the neo-pluralists are mostly political scientists, while the first group is made up mostly of sociologists.

demonstrating that they are highly influential. Thus Whitaker and Baxter "can boast of success in about 90 per cent of more than seventy-five . . . endeavors."[66] On a chance basis one would expect them to be on the winning side about half the time. How much of the difference can be attributed to Whitaker and Baxter? To find a satisfactory answer to questions like this is one of the most formidable problems of contemporary social science. Yet it is clear that no amount of description of techniques of influence will produce an answer.

Fortunately for the political scientist, the pay-off is usually a vote or election of some kind, a fact that would permit an imaginative use of election data to throw some light on the question. However, even where the pay-off is considered to be an election or a legislative vote, the more one moves away from direct to indirect techniques the more difficult it becomes to assess effects. How can we estimate the impact of institutional advertising on the attitudes of voters? How much of the generally favorable attitude of Americans toward business can be attributed to deliberate efforts to manipulate attitudes? Observers differ widely in appraising the extent to which business propaganda has actually influenced attitudes. In a characteristically astringent essay for *Fortune,* W. H. Whyte, Jr., concludes that the whole Free Enterprise campaign of American industry "is not worth a damn."[67] Mills argues the different but not necessarily conflicting point that the mass media are "among the most important of those increased means of power now at the disposal of elites of wealth and power."[68] Since one quickly begins to outstrip even the most advanced methods of analysis in trying to appraise the effects of indirect techniques, it might be argued that the subject should be dropped — at least by scholars, and at least temporarily. But the question probably can not be downed so cavalierly, since too much in the way of political theory (both normative and empirical) depends on the assumptions one

[66] Kelley, *op. cit.,* p. 43.

[67] "The Great Free Enterprise Campaign," in *Is Anybody Listening?* (New York, 1952), p. 7.

[68] Mills, *op. cit.,* p. 315. Cf. also V. Packard, *The Hidden Persuaders* (New York, 1957)

makes about the sources of political attitudes. To return to one of the extreme models referred to a moment ago, if one assumes that political preferences are simply plugged into the system by leaders (business or otherwise) in order to extract what they wish from the system, then the model of plebiscitary democracy is substantially equivalent to the model of totalitarian rule. There is probably no way at present of arriving at an adequately testable theory. If the question is to be dealt with at all, the theorist will need to exploit a broad range of investigatory techniques, factual materials, and intellectual disciplines ranging from historical studies to statistical analysis.

MOTIVES AND ATTITUDES

In recent years political scientists have begun to turn their attention once more to the political significance of motivations, character, attitudes, and ideologies — a topic that most political philosophers from Plato to Rousseau assumed, as a matter of course, to constitute a problem of central relevance to any comprehensive theory of politics. The appearance of Lane's *The Regulation of Businessmen* in 1954 reflected this resurgence of interest; fortunately for the subject we are concerned with in this essay, the book deals with the attitudes, values, and ideologies of businessmen and (to a lesser extent) bureaucrats. It is based mainly on a "series of studies — marginal between case studies and ordinary, if prolonged, interviews — of twenty-five busi-essmen in two New England states," a content analysis of the magazine *Connecticut Industry,* and a study of violations of regulatory law committed by the New England shoe industry.[69] Lane concludes that to the businessmen he studied the economic costs of regulation were relatively low; but the psychic costs were high. Regulation challenges the businessman's ideology, damages his self-image, generates frustrations by depriving him of customary choices, and creates anxieties by introducing new uncertainties into an already unpredictable environment. Further friction is generated between businessmen and bureau-

[69] R. E. Lane, *The Regulation of Businessmen, Social Conditions of Government Economic Control* (New Haven, 1954), pp. viii–ix.

crats because of differences in occupational traits, in the language they are accustomed to use, in standards of evaluation, and in their reference groups. It follows that among the important conditions for effective regulation of business are means for minimizing damage to the businessman's ego and changing businessmen's attitudes. But since the attitudes of businessmen are anchored in their group relations, the change must be through local communities (which differ markedly in attitudes toward regulation), business associations, and sympathetic occupational groups within the firm.[70]

It is too soon to say whether Lane's attempt to introduce a radically new perspective into the analysis of regulation will have the impact it deserves. But the rapid development of measures and scales for politically relevant attitudes opens up a whole new area of investigation that will almost certainly be exploited—if not by political scientists then (as is so often the case with questions of importance to the study of politics that have been neglected in the conventional organization of the discipline) by sociologists and psychologists.

While the study of the politically relevant attitudes and ideologies of businessmen can easily be assimilated into political science, the study of motivations can hardly move much faster than innovations in psychological theory and method permit. Nonetheless, even here there are some interesting new possibilities. N. Martin of the University of Chicago, in a still unpublished study, has made a comparison of certain kinds of motives in businessmen and government administrators. Some of the most intriguing possibilities along this line have been opened up by McClelland of Harvard and Atkinson of Michigan, who have developed measures of the relative strength of three motivations which they have called "need for achievement," "need for affiliation," and "need for power." In a dissertation in progress at Yale, J. Guyot is attempting to compare the strength of these motives among rising, middle-range executives in business and in government. Studies such as these will help to reduce the dependence on myths and impressions as a source of information about differences and

[70] *Ibid.*, pp. 19–20, 72, 121–27.

similarities between business bureaucrats and government bureaucrats.

Equally if not more important, of course, are the images of business and businessmen reflected in the attitudes and ideologies of various American publics. Many of the conventional assumptions contained in political lore — such as the relatively greater hostility of mid-Westerners to "Wall-Street" — have never been tested except by a kind of impressionistic content analysis of political propaganda. In 1951, however, the Survey Research Center of the University of Michigan published a study of public attitudes toward Big Business based on the responses of 1200 persons interviewed in 1950.[71] Although the findings of the survey are somewhat difficult to interpret, three things stand out fairly clearly: If there is any widespread hostility in this country to big business, it did not show up in the survey; almost no one seemed to be worried about the political power of big business; and the role of big business in American life was not a salient issue to most people. About 76 per cent of the respondents said that the good things about big business outweighed the bad. When they were asked to rank big businesses with "businesses that are not big," labor unions, the national government, and state governments according to their "influence on how things go in this country," 13 per cent put big business first, although only 3 per cent *desired* it to be in first place; another 23 per cent put it in second place, compared with only 13 per cent who wanted it to be in second place. Paradoxically, however, only 3 per cent seemed to feel that big business had too much power over institutions such as government, newspapers, and schools — and 53 per cent felt that some sort of government control over big business was a good thing. (Nearly half the sample put the relative "influence" of labor unions as in either first or second place, and three-quarters of them preferred labor unions to be in third, fourth, or fifth place.) Only 25 per cent seemed to display any emotional involvement in the issue; the issue of "big business" was much more likely to be salient to a member of the small

[71] The Survey Research Center, Institute for Social Research, University of Michigan, *Big Business from the Viewpoint of the Public* (Ann Arbor, 1951).

minority who disliked big business than to those who felt the good outweighed the bad.[72]

Now in this case as in most others we do not know nearly enough about the attitudes of people. What sorts of people, for example, make up that group to whom the issue of Big Business is salient: that is, those who not only have some information but some feelings on the matter? And what sorts make up that small minority of "radicals" to whom the issue is salient and who say that the bad things about big business outweigh the good? Are there important geographical differences in the distribution of attitudes? What *kinds* of influence do people perceive, and how do they respond to different kinds of perceived influence? Are individuals in positions of political leadership markedly different from others?[73]

One plausible conclusion, however, is that as with most public "issues" the role of business in American life is a matter of immediate concern to only a minority. It is extremely doubtful whether the problem of the "legitimacy" of the power of the large corporation in American life is meaningful to anyone outside a tiny group of perceptive observers like A. A. Berle.[74] Whether the active minority concerned with Big Business is significantly larger or smaller than the active minorities concerned with many other important policy areas, one can not say on the present evidence. So long as the performance of business measures up moderately well to expectations (as the Michigan study suggests it did in 1950), the problems associated with the roles of businessmen in American life are unlikely to occupy more than the sporadic attention of decision-makers and attentive publics. But if business fails again to meet popular expectations as dismally as it did in the decade after 1929, there is nothing in the src or other studies of opinion to suggest that public attitudes

[72] *Ibid.,* pp. 18, 20, 26, 44, 56.

[73] It is only fair to point out that the src study a) calls attention to some of these gaps (p. 134) and b) reports that census-type variables "do not seem to differentiate those seeing or desiring different order positions [i.e., in ranking Big Business with the other four institutions] to any significant degree." (p. 103).

[74] *Economic Power and the Free Society.*

would not shift rapidly and vengefully against business and produce extensive changes in the existing system of relations between business firms and the government.

What these changes might be, however — or even what a stable future is likely to hold in the way of evolutionary changes — is difficult to predict in the absence of any well-defined ideological alternatives, in the United States, to the present order. Paradoxically, the very absence of any competing ideology critical of business, reformist in mood, and deeply rooted in American beliefs and folkways, may be conducive to relatively violent and abrupt changes, should business performance ever again run sharply counter to popular expectations.[75]

Business Civilization and the Political Order

The capacious, far-ranging, reflective work of a civilized mind wrestling with the giant problems of an historical period is not usually reducible to a set of research papers. A concern for the relations between a business civilization and a popular political order has generated some of the most creative and influential writings of the past half century. One thinks at once of Tawney, Veblen, Weber, Schumpeter, Hayek, Fromm, Mannheim, Lippman, and Popper, to name only a few. Of

[75] Political scientists who teach courses and/or write textbooks on "government regulation of business," "public control of business enterprise," etc., might feel, with considerable justification, that they have been given short shrift in this section and indeed in the whole essay. Since I have been largely concerned with gaps in our knowledge, I have not stressed the one area where a good deal of work has been done, namely the operation of legal and administrative regulatory mechanisms. Standard works include M. Anshen and F. D. Wormuth, *Private Enterprise and Public Policy* (New York, 1954); M. E. Dimock *Business and Government* (New York, 3d ed., 1957); H. Koontz and R. W. Gable, *Public Control of Economic Enterprise* (New York, 1956); H. R. Smith, *Government and Business* (New York, 1958); M. Fainsod and L. Gordon, *Government and the American Economy* (rev. ed., New York, 1948; a new edition is under preparation by J. Palamountain); E. S. Redford, *Administration of National Economic Control* (New York, 1952), and his *Public Administration and Policy Formation* (Austin, 1956). Cf. also M. Fainsod, "The Study of Government and Economic Life in the United States," in *Contemporary Political Science* (Paris, UNESCO, 1950).

this particular group, it is significant that all were strongly influenced by the nineteenth-century view of "capitalism" and "socialism" as distinct, mutually exclusive, conflicting systems. Only two were American by birth and education. None can be classified as a professional political scientist, although economics, history, sociology, and philosophy are represented. Some of the problems these men were perturbed about seem no longer relevant. Others persist. New ones appear.

There is, certainly, no lack of questions for the social philosopher: What criteria ought we to use to appraise business performance? Are these consistent with the criteria we use to appraise performance in government? What are the consequences for American life, politics, attitudes, and civilization of American business behavior? How ought one to evaluate these consequences? How can the adverse consequences be minimized and the advantageous consequences maximized? Is our civilization consumption-oriented to a greater degree than others? If so, how is this related to business influences and needs? Do our commitments to the idea of maximizing individual consumption lead to a neglect of goods that can only be consumed or enjoyed jointly? Or to a relatively heavy emphasis on "material" as compared with "ideal" personal orientations? Does a business culture generate a relatively large amount of personal alienation, isolation, and anomie? Is the growth of the Organization Man a fact? If so, why? Does business competition help produce highly "competitive" personalities — or is this merely an illusory play on words?

Conversely, in what ways does the existence of the American political order influence the behavior of business? How, for example, does the political order affect the rate of economic growth? The allocation of resources? The distribution of incomes? What changes would be required in the political order for given changes in the rate of growth, or in the patterns of resource allocation or income distribution? How much did the political order contribute to the relatively high rate of growth over the past century? In what respects does it facilitate or impede our "competition" with the relatively high rate of growth in the USSR? How, if at all, is the political order related

to innovation and invention? Is the influence of corporate businessmen over economic decisions excessive? What decisions? And by
what criteria?

Are the old issues involved in the struggles over the regulation of
business, the welfare state, planning, and, in other countries, socialism
largely dead? If not, what is their current content? If so, what are the
new or future sources of tension generated in the relations of the political to the economic order?

And so on. There is no dearth of important and even urgent questions. But political scientists do not, by and large, seem to be search-
ing for answers.

BY MASON HAIRE

Psychology and the

Study of Business:

Joint Behavioral Sciences

Introduction

THERE is, of course, a close logical relationship between the study of business and the behavioral sciences. Indeed, the study of business *is* a behavioral science, studying a sample of behavior in a particular context. However, the flow of ideas and facts between the areas has not been as full and detailed as one might hope. This paper tries, for the field of psychology, to make the gap easier to cross.

The student of business tends to see problems in terms of the goals of the operation and within the confines of the industrial organization. He sees problems of production, control, evaluation, and management. The psychologist, not surprisingly, has tended to see psychological problems. Many of them have immediate and pressing relevance for the student of business, but their detail and relevance have not always been clear. The psychologist sees problems related to production—the nature of the productive performance, of the people who do it, and of the motivation to do it well or quickly. He sees the problems of management and control in the fields of communication, leadership, group effects, and the like. However, he sees them—and states them—as psychological problems, and, as such, they are not maximally available to students of business. I will try here to give a resume of some of these problems so that the current areas of research are clear, and so that the problems can be seen and understood as psychological problems against the context of psychological theory. I hope they will also be clear as problems of interest—and especially as possible research areas—to the student of business.

Generally, someone in Business Administration recognizes the existence of a field called Industrial Psychology, but the problems are seldom quite the ones he is interested in, and it is never entirely clear to him why psychologists attack just the areas they do. He recognizes the existence of some work on selection, though not the detailed bases of it. It seems both a little sterile and forbiddingly technical to him. Research on the design of equipment and operators' characteristics is, by and large, somewhat hazy to him. That belongs in the bailiwick of the industrial engineer. There is work on communication and groups which seems relevant, but the tremendous body of published material seems to make it unavailable. Lately the human relations movement has brought this material forcefully to bear on the business field, but—with the best entrepreneurial technique—with a kind of a *mystique* of its own that makes it almost impenetrable to the layman. Similarly in the field of motivation. It has become old-hat to attack the economists' grossly oversimplified economic man with a single (profit) motive, but in following it up, the psychologist seems to retreat into a mish-mash of Freudianism and a set of labels for motives that are, confusingly, at once common sense and bewilderingly esoteric.

What can be done? The student of business is a behavioral scientist. His lectures touch on these areas, his theoretical models demand assumptions about them, and his research leads him to the brink of them. Similarly, the psychologist has research interests and theoretical problems in the (large) sample of behavior represented by business and industry. The needs on both sides constitute the justification for a kind of a resume and reordering of some of the work relevant to the two disciplines.

I purposely say "some of the work." It would be much too long and detailed—and much too dull—to try to abstract the whole of the field of Industrial Psychology. This kind of exhaustive treatment can be found in a well-selected group of texts. Here, I have concentrated on a rough breadth, and on problems that seem a) crucial or essential to understanding the development of a field, b) areas where there is a good deal of research and theory going on at present, and

c) those where joint progress between the psychologist and the student of business seems possible and likely in the near future. Within these, I hope the present state and development of ideas becomes clear, and that sufficient references are given to enable the reader to follow them in detail on his own.

It seems especially relevant to try to show the relationship between the various social sciences and the field of business. It is a particularly fruitful field for interdisciplinary progress. This cross-fertilization so ardently desired in recent years seems to be relatively little effective when it is impressed from an external aim of unification. The psychologist and sociologist may be urged to lie down together like the lion and the lamb, but this kind of union has not been especially fruitful. The addition of the problems of business, however, adds a very different element. Now there are problems to focus the conceptual developments of the several fields. Importantly, these problems are grounded in an external area which has rules, processes, and pressures of its own which determine the foci. The theoretical power of the various approaches gains leverage by coming to grips with problems outside the field instead of flailing about in the somewhat solipsistic morass of the single discipline. The joint approach on common problems independently set from outside the fields seems likely to be the most fruitful ground for research and theory in the social sciences.

The General Characteristics of Industrial Psychology

In spite of its adjectival title, suggestive of an "applied" character, industrial psychology is and always has been primarily an academic discipline. Rooted in psychological concepts in individual differences, motivation, social and experimental psychology, its inception and the course of its development have been primarily determined by the developing nature of psychological theory, rather than the pressures of exigencies within business and industry. The business of applying psychology to industry has been the application of psychology as it developed as psychology, rather than a reshaping of the field by industrial pressures. To be sure, outside developments are evident in the history of industrial psychology. The development of the Civil Service gave impetus to studies of merit rating and of selection. The creation of collective bargaining initiated a whole new set of psychological problems, and the complexities of war-time equipment spurred human engineering studies. More recently, the increase in size of organizations, the tight labor market which put emphasis on non-financial incentives, and the increasing rationalization of jobs gave prominence to a set of social psychological problems.

External pressures have had an influence, but the development has been primarily within the sub-field and within psychology. It is in these terms that this paper will try to draw the developing lines. The main determinants seem to be growths within the general body of psychological thinking in major areas such as motivation, individual differences, and the like. Within this framework there are a separate set of narrower, more specific sub-fields of industrial psychology itself which have a developmental history of their own. Finally, cutting across these are the historical developments outside the field which exert a special influence from time to time.

It seems useful to distinguish three traditions within the field. They have quite different conceptual bases, their developmental histories are not at all the same, and they have relatively little contact with one another. The first is the field of personnel psychology, flowing from the tradition of individual differences; the second is human engineering, growing out of applied experimental psychology; and the third is less compact, what might be called industrial social psychology, although it includes some individual problems of motivation and the like.

The first two—personnel psychology and the human engineering approach—stand sharply apart. Personnel psychology comes from the tradition of differential psychology—the study of the differences between people. It focuses, for example, on how widely particular skills and abilities are distributed within a group of people, which of them seem to appear together in a single person, and how, in clusters of such abilities, one person will tend to differ from another. It is the tradition of the intelligence test, where, typically, the attention was focused on the measurement of a particular ability, its distribution among people, and its correlation with other behaviors. The human engineer, on the other hand, comes from the experimental tradition. His problems tend to be phrased in "if . . . then" terms—the classical experimental language of the dependent and the independent variable. These statements tend to be of the form, "Behavior A depends on prior condition B. If I create condition B behavior A will result." He observes the average effect of the condition on a group exposed to it, and measures the difference from an unexposed group. He is not interested in the individual's behavior; individual behavior is a nuisance, a contribution to variance around the mean.

The approach from the side of individual differences, applied to industry, seeks to identify the best man for the job. It uses essentially a correlational method and viewpoint, and the attention is focused on within-group variance in sharp distinction to the human engineer whose main interest is in the between-group variance, or the effects of treatments. The aim of the engineer is not to find the *right* man for the job, but as Chapanis (26) says, "to make the job fit the man—any man." Cronbach puts the distinction well (31) when he says the experimentalist attacks nature, seeking to modify the environment, while the correlationist approaches nature like a lover, taking her as she is and studying her as such. There is more than a deep conceptual difference between them; they are diametrically opposed in practice. Every step of success the engineer has in making the job fit Everyman destroys part of the reason for being of the selection tester, who depends on the fact that *not* everyone can do the job equally well. In the reverse direction, it is also true, but less compelling, that if the effectiveness of selection had been greater it would have left less room for the work of the human engineer. This is not quite so true as the obverse, since the design of equipment would always be useful in special situations—where the task required skills which were in scarce supply, in a tight labor market, or in a military situation where the characteristics of the labor force may be inflexible, and the demands of the equipment beyond much improvement by classification. In a way it is strange that the liberal tradition of remaking the world to make it fit Man better, in contrast with the relatively passive caste-ridden Darwinian approach of the correlationist, should come from something called Engineering psychology. The social philosophy seems to be grounded less in ideological conviction, however, than in a response to the complexities and demands of equipment.

The philosophy of the social theorist is a little harder to put concisely than the other two, but he stands quite far apart from them. The historical background is more complex. It includes some sociological traditions and a group of diverse psychological fields. The classic Management and the Worker (Roethlisberger and Dickson, 74) marked the clear emphasis on certain aspects of group structure and social motivation.

Moreno and the sociometric tradition contributed the interest in the internal structure of the group—the relations among the members. Lewin and the group dynamicists focused on the forces and tensions in the group, attending to its dynamic equilibrium rather than its static structure. Some of the philosophy of the instinctivists has remained in the interest in motivation and attitude measurement, and the communication theorists, in dealing with both structure and process, draw on a variety of fields. There is a phenomenological trend apparent as the field of social perception is brought to bear on industrial problems. In some ways the social approach seems closer to that of the engineer than to the correlationist. Both the social psychologist and the human engineer aim at saying how the job might be rebuilt to maximize the utilization of human potential. They both tend to see behavior as caused by the context in which it is imbedded. The correlationist sees behavior flowing from the characteristics of individuals with the variance produced by the situations in which they find themselves. Both the engineer and the social psychologist see the behavior produced by situations, with the variance attributable to individual differences. They will both seek to modify behavior by modifying the conditions determining it. The social theorist, however, turns from the relatively simple sensory and motor problems and seeks to manipulate quite different variables. He will see advance in building work situations to provide maximum motivational satisfactions, groups structured so that their strengths are not barriers but aids to the accomplishment of the organization's productive objectives, and the like.

These, briefly, are the three sub-areas we will consider. Let us look at each of them for a little of the conceptual history and the research problems they contain.

Human Engineering

Historically, the human engineering approach is probably best traced to the early "conditions of work" interest. Here, notably, the very general environment was the center of attention in studies of fatigue, lighting, effects of music, and the like. The plant tended to be the unit of variation and the work group the unit of response. In their original design, the Hawthorne studies (Roethlisberger and Dickson, 74) followed this pattern as late as the 1930s. They sought to study the effect of rest pauses, wage rates, and the like—as conditions—on the behavior of a selected group. Later, attention in the field narrowed to a more nearly individual basis. Although it does not quite fit chronologically, the spirit of the time studies of Taylor and the motion studies of Gilbreth helped to serve to narrow the interest to smaller processes.

The present interest—for example, in equipment design—uses the individual as the unit of response analysis and some intimate contact-apparatus as the unit of controlled variation. The work begins with simple questions like, "how long should the handle of the crank be?" and "how big should the type be?" and goes on to much subtler problems of psycho-motor control and the display of information. Methodologically, a real advance was made by the emphasis on the identification of error variance associated respectively with man and machine in complex systems.

The basic approach of the engineering psychologist has been to ask, "what abilities does man have?", "what does the end product require?", and "how can the machine be built to go between the two?" It has some interesting pressures from implications for the social system outside of psychology. It fits in well with the general tendency to rationalize jobs in the interest of minimizing the cost of turnover. If the job could be built "to fit the man—any man," it also made it easier for the industrial organization to absorb variations attendant on business cycles by hiring and firing relatively homogeneous personnel units requiring a minimum of recruitment and training. As the development popularly called automation continues—the control of machines by machines—the picture changes. As Drucker (36) points out, with the high cost of automation the area of business risk shifts. It becomes important to stabilize production—preferably at maximum output, but importantly at a stable figure. The area of psychological research interest tends to shift from the producer to the consumer. As a stable volume of production becomes important to amortize fixed costs of expensive machinery, it is no longer possible to take advantage of peaks and valleys of demand by hiring and firing. What is needed is an understanding of consumer behavior, on the one hand, and product design, on the other. Ideally, one wants a product served by a high inclination to purchase, engineered with rapid obsolescence—not necessarily mechanical obsolescence. Motivational obsolescence will do, as the auto industry shows us. The psychological insight needed to make automation work is the definition of a product with a fast waning of interest in it after purchase and an equally fast rise in the desire to buy another model.

The rationalization of jobs to fit Everyman has had implications in both the other sub-areas of industrial psychology. On the one hand, to the extent to which individual differences are minimized, the individual's feeling of his peculiar contribution is reduced, and this diminution in egoistic need-satisfactions has formed a fair part of the interest of the industrial social psychologist. On the other hand, the rationalization of jobs for Everyman is a tremendous waste of existing individual differences, though the correlationists have not made an issue of it. De-skilling benefits companies taken singly, but to maximize national productivity, it would seem wiser to utilize the peaks of individual abilities rather than the mid-height of the mean. By and large, also, though it is not a necessary implication, the

changes resulting from human engineering have not maximally utilized the potential effects of training. In general, equipment has been
designed so people can *do* jobs better. It could be designed so they
could *learn* to do them better, or, a quite different problem, so they
could learn better to do them. Although there is no necessary limitation in the viewpoint of the human engineer, these two problems have
been largely neglected. We will see, later, that the correlationist has
similarly turned away from learning as a variable.

The human engineer has also begun to challenge the basis of the
traditional industrial engineer. In a sense, the engineer first invaded the
field of the psychologist by recommending certain behavioral procedures on the basis of the findings of time and motion studies. This
approach, however, traditionally treats the machine as a constant and
man as a variable, exploring the optimal movements most suitable to
the continued operation of a particular machine. Except for studies of
plant lay-out and work-bench lay-out, the engineer has typically
sought to change the worker. Engineering psychology, since it is a
planning of the machine on the basis of the operator's characteristics,
was bound to challenge this approach. A beginning of such a challenge can be seen, for example, in J. S. Brown and W. O. Jenkins'
paper (20) in which they propose a reclassification of motor responses into static reactions, positioning reactions, and movement reactions. These are not divided in terms of observed performance on a
job, like, for example, the "carry empty" "carry loaded" categories
of the Therblig notation, but rather are based on hypothesized characteristics of the operator, and, as such, would provide an entirely different approach to the problem of time and motion study. Likewise,
Birmingham and Taylor (17) also suggest ways to analyze performances which lead to entirely different kinds of categories from the
Therblig. Although it has not developed fully, the viewpoint has the
seed of a broadly different approach to work methods. It would search
for categories in the characteristics of behavior, and taking these as
givens, flesh out the general principles on which machines could be
designed to utilize them.

Specific empirical research areas in the field have, in general, fallen under three heads: studies of the optimal environment, studies of information display, and studies of equipment design (Fitts, 40). It is in the nature of the field that the published reports are highly specific and tend to have a fragmentary character whose integration is only achieved through an overview of the concepts of the whole field. The volume of published reports on individual determinations is tremendous, even outside of the conventional professional journals. The Navy, for example, in 1955 published (U.S. Navy Special Devices Center, 90) a bibliography of 376 references to unclassified project reports in these areas.

One problem within the area has shown tremendous growth and seems to have the broadest possible implications for future research. Chapanis, Garner, and Morgan (27) gave a clear and extended treatment to the problem of kinds and sources of error in man-machine systems. The identification of constant and variable errors and of errors associated with the man and the equipment early gave the human engineer a kind of diagnostic tool to identify the places where work would be most profitably applied. Subsequently, this kind of approach lead to an analysis of systems errors in which all the specific problems of the field converged: the design of the controls may maximize or minimize the variability of the operator's response, the display of information similarly influences the error, and the serial order of responses within an operator or from operator to operator become important variables.

It is worthwhile spending a little time on the question of error. The tradition of the physical sciences (and most of the biological) has been to neglect error—typically a phenomenon is measured once, or, perhaps two or three times, and the average is taken to be a value. Repeated measures are treated for the average, or central tendency, but, by and large, no attention is paid to the variability around that average, or dispersion. The behavioral scientist, on the other hand, finds variability a major characteristic of his data, and one of the major contributions of the experimental method of phychologists has been refinements in dealing with error. Indeed, in the case of "just noticeable differences" (limens or thresholds), for example, it has been possible in a sense to create something out of nothing, and to identify a stable phenomenon whose defining characteristic is error variation.

Engineers, in the same tradition as the physical scientists, have tended to take a single measurement as *the* value, and the result has often been micrometers, gauges, controls, and measuring instruments with a sensitivity far higher than is warranted in view of the error introduced by the operator reading them. In this case, we are referring only to the error of reading, not to the size of the class interval appropriate for use. For example, few of us can read a vernier micrometer accurately. In some cases, if we could do so the information would be intelligible. Here the important error variance is in the reading. On the other hand, the thermometer on our cars often gives a whole range of temperature values. Most of us can read the gauge fairly accurately, but we don't know what to do with the information. A simple "yes-no" gauge would do. Here the grossness of the class interval is in the information system.

When we first begin to see error in performance data, variable and constant errors stand out immediately. To illustrate the two, if one were testing a rifle and found all the shots went through the same hole but two inches above the bull's-eye, there would be zero variable error and plus two inches constant error. Fortunately constant errors are little problem. For one thing, they typically mean a simple adjustment of the mechanism to bring the center of impact to perfect performance. Further, the mathematics of error addition is such that unless the constant error is about $\frac{1}{3}$ of the variable error, its influence on the total error will be negligible.

The analysis of variable errors is more interesting. In any man-machine system, part of the variability around the mean is associated with the man and part with the machine. For example, in a radar ranging system, the standard deviation associated with the operator may be 20 yards, and that associated with the machine 10 yards. Since variable errors accumulate by adding variances (squared standard deviations), the two errors combine to produce a total error of 22.36 yards. If it were possible to eliminate all the error from the machine, it would reduce the error by 2.36 yards, or about 10%. On the other hand, if instead of trying to eliminate every vestige of error from the machine, we tried by training to improve the operator by 25%—to reduce his error from 20 yards to 15—we would accomplish the same result. If we could cut the operator error in half we would reduce the total error by about 42%; if we cut the machine error in half we would reduce the total error by about 16%. Such an analysis points clearly to the area where it is economical to work for improvement. As a final product becomes the result of a linkage of several men and several machines, the same kind of an analysis helps diagnose where effort will be efficient in more complex cases. Where several models of the same machine produce independently instead of a linked system, appropriate experimental design allows the same estimate of error associated with man and machine.

As this tendency to analyze complex man-machine systems in terms of minimizing systems errors grows, the engineer approaches a field which seems, at first glance, to belong more properly in the bailiwick of the social theorist: the problem of organization theory. Within relatively small units—radar warning systems, fire-control systems, and the like—this approach has designated the optimal organization for minimizing error in the system. As it would apply to a larger organization—for instance, a business or an industry group—the work would be cumbersome and voluminous, and it would require some new techniques for the descriptions of activities in various parts, but eventually an organization theory for industry should flow from the approach of the human engineer. With its history of concentration on the display of information and of characteristic responses to certain kinds of messages, it probably fits most harmoniously with the decision theorists' work on theories of teams (Helmer, 51; Marschak, 66; Radner, 73). The introduction of problems of uncertainty in such systems (Carter, Meredith, and Shakle, 23) changes the problem considerably from the usual formulation of the human engineer, but still somewhat paradoxically, one basis for a future theory of social organizations seems to lie in the field. It is perhaps worth pointing out that the approach from the analysis of systems error in complex man-machine systems gives a particular kind of organization—i.e., one that minimizes error—and that it will differ sharply from the social theorist who may, for example, be interested also in maximizing personal and organizational goals simultaneously.

Personnel Psychology

In its simple base, the field of personnel psychology rests on a correlational relationship between a normally distributed predictor variable (which may or may not be simply related to the skills and abilities required on the job) on the one hand, and another normally distributed measure of criterion performance. The equally simple matching task is to eliminate, on the basis of the relatively inexpensive predictor variable, those with low likelihood of success in criterion performance.

As the field developed, all three—the predictor, the criterion, and the match—lost their simplicity. The predictor went from simple motor skills and primary mental abilities to job knowledge, and finally to interests, motives, background, and even trainability. The criterion broadened into the complexities of job families, job description, job evaluations, merit ratings, and multi-dimensionality, and has become the knottiest problem in the field. Matching went from the simple mathematics of screening to the much more involved problems of classification and team construction.

In some ways the outstanding fact in the history of the simple selection procedures is the relatively long plateau of no real progress after a period of initial improvement. Cronbach (31) puts it that none of the refinements since 1920 have improved practical predictors by a noticeable amount. This is a rather extreme view, but it certainly seems likely that if one could plot all the validity coefficients ever reported, they would probably form a characteristic learning curve, with a rapid initial rise and a long plateau as validities settle below an unattainable asymptote of .40 or .45.

Hull, in 1928 (55) suggested that a practical limit for validities might be in the neighborhood of .50. Nothing in the history of selection testing has radically revised this figure after thirty years. The main source of limitation, however, seems to be with the proper and adequate definition of the criterion variable rather than with either the predictor or the nature of the match. It is almost certain that here, as in other areas referred to in this paper, further differentiation of the criterion is the eventual path to research progress. Wallace and Weitz (95) pointed out in 1955 that the criterion problem leads all other topics in industrial psychology in lip service, but trails in work reported. The problem is especially difficult in this area.

The two problems of relevancy and reliability of criterion measures are relatively straight forward. The problem of the identification of multiple criteria and their subsequent combination and weighting is probably the most difficult but the most fruitful. The so-called "dollar" criterion, or the simple criterion of productivity seems inevitably to hide the details of the psychological problem involved. On the one hand, such criteria leave out other important relevant measures—e.g., turnover, grievances, etc. On the other hand, and perhaps more important, such criteria are themselves so determined by a multitude of factors (various skills and abilities, motivations, working conditions, and the like) that their prediction will probably never go far beyond the present level. If we were content to identify, in an individual, the motor skills necessary to high production, the problem would be simple. However, this criterion is not enough. We need a man who will be at work to do the producing, we need quality production, and other things depending on the job. Each of these could be identified as a criterion—production, absenteeism, scrap-loss, etc.—and separately predicted. With individual tests for each, a battery could be made, weighted by the regression weights of such, with a single multiple correlation somewhat higher than any of the individuals. One part of the job is here. The identification of elements in the criterion and their assembly with proper weights in a multiple criterion.

Another source of difficulty lies in the complex determination, on the side of the individual, of the criterial performance. Beside the abilities needed to produce, we should, ultimately, identify the capacity for sustained motivation to produce, and the like. Only the detailed differentiation of the criterion and its eventual reconstitution seem to hold promise for raising the general level of validities.

The problem of classification—optimizing the simultaneous match of several men and several positions—has been a difficult one. Thorndike (87) began the mathematics for a simple case, and, more recently, iterative solutions of the linear programming type have shown promise. Here, also, the maximization of the matrix values, while a great advance, can never be better than the criterion used to scale the values concerned.

There is one other problem in the balance between selection and classification. Selection on a company level becomes classification on a national level. If Company A needs a man with skill S, it competes with all the other people who need that skill. Ideally, the traditional operation of a laissez-faire economy will resolve these competitions in the national interest. The whole economy will operate in the fashion of a computer attempting an iterative solution of a matrix with person by person maximization. Several differences appear, however. For one thing, the labor market is notoriously slower than the computer; mobility is determined by many other forces than economic advantage. Institutional forces—unions, pension plans, and the like—also damp the process. Finally, the failure to make the classification explicit in this type of solution leaves us very little prepared for national mobilization in an emergency. Behavioral skills are among the most difficult scarce resources to identify and allocate. An explicit attention to the problem in relatively less critical periods would facilitate it.

Even more discouraging in the mathematics of simple selection are the implications of a paper by Brown and Ghiselli (19) which is too little noticed in the field. Working within the simple algebraic relationships of the correlation between predictor and criterion, they provide a set of values in which one may read the per cent improvement in productivity of a selected over an unselected population. The improvement depends on a) the validity, b) the per cent selected from the applicants, and c) the variance in criterial performance before selection. Putting in hypothetical but reasonable figures, the result is discouraging. Given a frequently encountered validity of, say, .30,

and the ability to reject 50% of the applicants (having already rejected on all other bases but the test), and with a ratio of best to worst
in the criterion of 1.5 to 1 (one way to describe the variance in
criterial performance), the improvement in productivity of the selected group over the unselected will be only about 3%. Even 3% is
not to be disregarded as a practical matter, but it is not the universal
panacea that many business men have dreamed of—a dream that
many psychologists, who should have known better, have encouraged.

Several specific implications seem to flow from the Brown and
Ghiselli paper. For one thing, in practical terms, the tremendous leverage gained by shifting the cut-off is obviously related to the state of
the labor market. In the past few years we have had a very tight labor
market where it was necessary to hire almost everyone to fill jobs.
Now, with the war-time bulge in the birth-rate coming out of schools,
considerably more selectivity is possible, and the practical value of
even relatively low validities increases. We should note, also, that
these values refer to a simple yes-no selection, and do not take into
account the more complicated classification problem.

Again, the tendency to rationalize jobs mentioned above cuts across
the selector's effectiveness. No precise data are available on the ratio
of best to worst in industrial practice, but in highly mechanized pro-
duction-line situations the ratio is said to be about 1.1 to 1. Such a
value gives little power to selection. As this trend continues in the
interest of reducing the cost of turnover and training, the possible improvements by selection disappear. It is just here that the human engineer's attempt to rebuild the job so all can do it equally well comes
in direct conflict with the tester.

One area of testing probably benefits from two of the variables in
the Brown and Ghiselli function—personality tests and the so-called
assessment techniques for the early identification of high-level talent.
Although the validities are typically much lower, the variance of performance in, for example, executives, is very much greater than in
lathe operators, and the per cent selected is very much smaller as the
triangle of the hierarchy narrows toward the top. These last two
factors combine to outweigh the present validities and give much

more power than in the case of selection for clerical and manual jobs. In the present practical situation there is one special danger here. Many of the tests used for personality assessment in the interests of selecting executives are general personality tests which are not validated for executive performance but for the identification of personality traits. The relevance of these characteristics to successful performance is often made by a kind of intuitive judgment of what kind of person one would like to have on the job. Since it is impossible to forecast the demands that will be placed on the organization in the future, this seems to be a dangerous putting of all of one's personnel eggs in one basket. Fortunately, at the present, the validities are low enough so that the consistent use of almost any of the personality tests will still provide enough error variance to protect the organization against poor judgment about the qualities it thinks it is selecting.

The increase in productivity afforded by selection also leads one to think of the possible improvement offered by training. Unfortunately, the literature on the measured effect of training programs in industry is sparse. This is particularly surprising, perhaps, in a science where such a large proportion of research and theoretical development has been in the field of learning. Like the criterion problem, a great deal is said about the advisability of studying training, but relatively little has been done. Still, it does not seem over-optimistic to hope for considerably more than the 3–5% improvement offered by most selection tests.

There are some studies of the effectiveness of training showing positive results (Maier, 64; McGehee and Livingston, 68; Wallace and Twitchell, 94) and some showing no effect (Baxter, Taaffe, and Hughes, 16); again the criterion problem is an ever-present difficulty. Several studies have referred the effect of treatment back to a somewhat vague determinant known as the "climate" of the group or organization (Buchele, 21; Fleishman, 41; Jennings, 57). In the absence of precise definition of the variable or the way in which it operates, this has not proved fruitful, although it probably points to something which must be dealt with later. Certainly much of our training in industry takes place within a classroom, is measured there, and probably never shows an effect on the work-room floor (Fleishman, 41; Haire, 49).

Edgerton (37) suggests some solid advances in the field—"watch and do" training films, the Air Force work on team training, the Navy's work on where training devices are needed. In addition, the growth of the National Training Laboratory and the Western Training Laboratory have focused the group dynamicists' interest on the problem. Still, there is very little in the way of evaluation of the effectiveness of training.

There are a number of exhortatory articles urging an evaluation of training but relatively few comparable to Edgerton's in detail of review and research suggestion. He proposes a detailed research program including measurement of predictor abilities, variation of training methods, and criterion measures. In this way it is somewhat similar to Cronbach's proposal (31) that a matrix containing both treatments (training methods) and aptitudes is needed and that the interaction factors may be maximally effective. It should be pointed out that the approach implied in these two suggestions is, to some extent, at odds with the pure correlationists' approach outlined earlier, and is a step toward a rapprochement with the experimentalist. This combination of treatment and individual differences has not been explored in terms of job design and equipment, but there is no reason why it should not be.

For example, micro-motion techniques are well worked out for studying job performance. A detailed study of the way work is done by individuals high on the predictor and low on the criterion (or vice versa) might yield real possibilities for the redesign of performance leading to the productive criterion. Particularly when the ability required is scarce, such a procedure would be useful. In terms of the national productivity, a national sample of, for instance, psycho-motor skills and the redesign of jobs to take advantage of them would seem both feasible and fruitful.

The problem of training cuts across the selection problem more directly. Most validation studies are conducted against a fixed training criterion, i.e., the simple pass-fail criterion. However, we have little research on the prediction of trainability in terms of the correlation between a selector and the slope of the learning curve. In many cases a lower slope and a higher eventual level seems a real possibility, and for long employment the prediction of both slope and eventual improvement seems important. Again, most validities are against proficiency criteria taken very early in job-life compared to the typical tenure of a producer. There is some evidence that validities and intercorrelations taken at different periods of employment would give very different weightings in a predictive battery, and Fleishman (42) has suggested a change in the factorial content of motor skills with practice. In specific terms, these possibilities suggest that even our present validities—discouraging though they are—may be misleadingly over-optimistic. In the first case, for example, let us suppose we have a typical selection screening situation. A test for skill A has been shown to correlate .45 with the first months performance on job X, while a test for skill B correlates only .20. If, however, after six months or a year, skill B shows the high relation, we will have selected the wrong people. The second case has to do with the weighting of skills. Early in job performance, skills A and B may be weighted equally. Selection may be made on this basis since the validation was done on the first few months of production. If, later, the weightings of the two skills in the more practiced performance are 80/20 we will again have the wrong people. We should have taken the 80/20 type and put up with early poorer performance to get the later benefit. There is some evidence that both of these situations occur in part. All of these points seem to suggest that in addition to differentiation of the predicted criterion in terms of job-relevant factors the elaboration of its psychological components might also be fruitful.

In practical terms, the interview is still the most widely used selective device. Some progress has been made in the development of patterned interviews, biographical data blanks, and job knowledge tests to support the interviewer, but both because of its wide use and relatively little development, this area seems particularly ripe for research. The direction of development in terms of a validation of the interviewer himself on an actuarial basis seems the likeliest to bear fruit. The study

of the interviewer and validating him as an instrument is surprisingly
lacking in published research.

This brief statement has not included any reference to a group of the
classical topics in personnel psychology, such as fatigue, safety, merit
rating and performance evaluation, and the like. They are areas characteristic of the field, but they do not seem to me to be either crucial to
its logic or filled with promise of exciting research problems in the
near future. Consequently these, like many others, must go by without any real treatment at this time.

Industrial Social Psychology

As has been suggested above, it is harder to give a compact historical
background for this sub-area than for the others. An historical review
has recently been given elsewhere (Haire, 45) and will not be repeated
here. Likewise, it is harder in this area to give the central theme that
characterizes the field. Several of them must be identified; they will
be dealt with in detail below. The first of them is the interest in group
processes flowing from the impact of Lewin, Moreno, and the Mayo
school. These include the interest in sociometric structure of the group,
roles, resistance to change, small group dynamics, and the social
organization of the factory. The second is an interest in "the psychology of the other one" in the *verstehen* tradition, with an emphasis
on an approach through perception and a detailed understanding of
the world of experience of the subject. A third is the presence of a
broad humanistic value which seems to run through the field. It is
often not explicit, but lurks immediately below the surface. For example, the "human relations" point of view often seems to suggest
that an increase in need satisfactions at work will increase productivity
(Brayfield and Crockett, 18); often, however, it seems as if the suggestion is that even though it may not increase productivity, an increase in need satisfactions for the worker is a social good. Argyris
(4) and others (Katz and Kahn, 58) seem to imply a similar calculus:
it is possible and advisable to reduce the achievement of organizational
goals in order to increase the achievement of individual need satis-

factions. A fourth stream in the field is a shifting in the manner of dealing with motivation. Taylorism and the vogue of incentive pay systems is closely related to the 18th century economic man. With more sophisticated psychological theory of motivation this interpretation gives way to one in which the drives are both more differentiated and internalized. Katz and Kahn (58) emphasize the internalization of reward. The differentiation of motives is more complex. In a sense the idea of economic man first gave way to a refined instinct theory. Veblen's *Instinct of Workmanship* (91), Tead's *Instincts in Industry* (86), and Williams' *Mainsprings of Man* (100) are early examples of the transitional state. Brayfield and Crockett (18) point to, and Kornhauser and Sharp (61) illustrate, the period when the instinct argument was being fragmented into complex motivational analyses and attitude surveys. With motivational sophistication, the complexities of modern theory appear, with, for example, Maier's emphasis on frustration (65), Stagner's interest in the conflict of dual allegiance (85), and the somewhat Freudian analysis of McGregor and others (69).

External influences have been particularly pressing in this area. The growth in size of industrial organizations has tended to destroy managerial reliance on old face-to-face relationships and to force a consideration of small group pressures and of formal characteristics of large organizations. The influence of rationalization of jobs has been mentioned; a reduction of emphasis on individual skill raises problems related to the kind of satisfactions one finds at work. It has also cut across the problem of group structure; for example, the disappearing role of the foreman is partly due to the changing organization of skills and responsibility. Collective bargaining has introduced new group problems of primary allegiances, and a rich field for attitude study as well as the in-process study of the bargaining itself. The union and its structure has become a subject for study, quite apart from its relation to management.

In addition to these there are some broad social currents related to the developments in industry. One of these is the increasing professionalization of management which means more than a simple speciali-

zation of function. It is the development of a group of specialists not
primarily related to the product, or, indeed, to production, but to the
administration of large complex social organizations and, especially, to
the problems of dealing with people within them. Partly out of this
has grown an interest in a proper philosophy of management—an
asking of "why" instead of the traditional "how" which should lead
the field to the broader problems of social philosophy. As the corporation grew, social psychological problems arose from the size. In
addition, however, problems arose from the fact that the legal entity
of the corporation and its traditional forms of organization were
frozen when size, communication technology, distribution technology, and automation of production were entirely different. In
many ways, industry has been less flexible in adapting its organization
to relevant technological changes in administration than other large
social organizations such as the Armed Services. This inflexibility
creates problems of its own. Still another general social interest arising
out of industrial organization is the current concern with conformity.
The *Organization Man* (98) makes contact with, but did not initiate,
the psychological research now going on in the field (Asch, 5; Crutchfield, 32; Tuddenham, 89). Finally, a whole group of basic societal
values related to industry seem to have shifted, and to have had an
influence on the general trends of interest in industrial social psychology. It used to be said that the United States was a success-oriented
culture, with values seated in productivity, industriousness, and
achievement. It is perhaps not excessive to say that it is becoming an
adjustment-oriented culture, with values seated in fitting in with the
group. We find contradictory norms of conformity and inconspicu-
ousness, on the one hand, inhibiting the individual from the single-
minded following of his own path, and, on the other hand, a rejection
of industriousness as compulsive and achievement-oriented. In this
connection, it is often said, jokingly, that the Ford Motor Co. has
grown so that if "old Henry" were alive today there would be no
place for him in the organization. It is probably true, and his inability
to fit in perhaps would stem from both of the values mentioned. Some
of this has been due to the influence of psychological thinking; some

of the psychological thinking about industrial problems is, in turn, influenced by it. In any case, the field clearly feels the impact of these historical developments within industry and society.

LARGE GROUP ORGANIZATION

In dealing with the problems related to group processes and structures, it is probably convenient to differentiate between large groups and small groups. Although there is really no fixed borderline between them, divergent interest seems clear. Historically, the interest in large group organization in industrial social psychology stems from the viewpoint of Elton Mayo, and particularly from the major report of Roethlisberger and Dickson (74). Mayo's insistence that "man's desire to be continuously associated . . . with his fellows is a strong, if not the strongest human characteristic" (Viteles, 92, p. 181) leads off in the direction of social motives and small group processes, but his interest "in the social organization of the factory" began an emphasis on the industrial organization as an autonomous macrocosmos. Within it there is an interest in role problems and motivations for broad functionally defined classes, e.g., the white collar worker, (Mills, 71), and in stresses within the structure of the organization such as the relation between staff and line (McGregor, 69). The hierarchical character of the organization appears in connection with prestige and status (Barnard, 12), though, surprisingly, it has not extended much into the studies of communication, where one might expect to find hierarchical barriers to the flow of information within the group. In contrast to the formal organization, the informal organization which develops spontaneously out of the group itself has been seen as a source for individual need satisfactions denied by the formal structure (Selznick, 78). The informal organization is also the basis for several studies of rumor and communication (Back, Festinger, Hymovitch, Kelley, Schacter, and Thibault, 7; Festinger, 39), and of morale in general (Arensberg, 3).

In dealing with the large group, the field of organization theory has shown great activity in recent years (Argyris, 4; Bakke, 8; Bakke, 9; Bakke and Argyris, 10; Barnard, 13; Haire, 47; Herbst, 52; Simon,

82; Simon, 83; Simon, 84; Weiss, 96). The most frequent single psychological thread running through this material is the conflict between the organization's goal and the satisfaction of the individual's motives. Is it possible to have unity of direction in an organization without sacrificing autonomy in the individual? Is it possible to have an hierarchical chain of command without sacrificing egoistic need satisfactions in the lower rungs? Is it possible to have planned rationalized production without sacrificing active independence? McGregor (69) suggests that it is. Argyrus (4), following a similar line, suggests that it is, but only at the cost of the organization's objectives. It is not perfectly clear in Argyris' treatment whether, on the one hand, he is dealing with the large organization, and the impeding effects of policies, rules, roles, and formal nets, or, on the other hand, with the more intimate geography of the small groups, and what Walker and Guest (93) call "mass production as a code of law." Barnard and Selznick (13 and 78) both find some solution in the existence of the informal organization to solve this problem. Simon (84) and the decision theorists in general tend to disregard the conflict, assuming a rational man, in many ways a more sophisticated counterpart of the old-fashioned economic man. He now maximizes strategies by relying on subjective evaluations and probabilities, but the original utility notion is not far submerged.

This conflict between the individual's goals and the organization's is part of the emphasis on broad humanistic values mentioned above. It is often urged that the individual should be provided with more motivational satisfaction. Sometimes it is explicitly held that an increase in his satisfactions will make a more effective producer. Sometimes it seems to be implicit that more satisfaction for the individual would be a Good Thing in any case; this is particularly true in dealing with socially valued satisfactions such as self-actualization, autonomy, and the like. In dealing with the industrial situation, this problem, which reappears in dealing with attitudes and motivation, remains unsolved. Under the heading of organization it is often suggested that the organization be operated in such a way that the individual's and the organization's achievement of goals be maximized simultaneously.

If this means that there is some ideal form of organization which can simultaneously bring about the absolute maxima of both at the same time it is never explicitly stated. If it means, as it often seems to, that some of the organization's goals should be sacrificed to increase the individual's, the calculus is never made specific, nor is the social philosophy on which it rests made explicit. In current approaches, the other possibility—that the individual's goals should be further sacrificed to increase the organization's—seldom seems even to lie beneath the surface. This is probably because in the last twenty years we have been in a very productive economy with relatively full employment, in which attention is directed less toward additional material output than to human values. Whatever the reason, the social psychologist unwittingly becomes a social philosopher as he chooses values underlying his analyses; the issues in the field would be clearer if these social philosophies were developed and made explicit.

Organization interest has turned to the relation between structure and function (Haire, 47; Weiss, 96), and Herbst (52) has reported some data applying an input-output analysis to the description of social organizations. In many ways the most surprising thing in the field of organization theory is the paucity of empirical data. For example, there seem to be no empirical histories of the growth of organizations in terms relevant to the social psychologist. In industry and economics there are a host of reports on growth and organization in terms of invested capital, dollar volume, and the like, but it is hard to find a history in terms of the number of people, what their functions were, their relations with one another, and the relative growth-rates of the parts and the whole. Such studies seem an essential base for organization theories if they are ever to move beyond the kind of possibility-spinning that characterizes them today.

In many ways, the interest in organization theory is a particularly apt example of the interdisciplinary focus of many of the social sciences. It broadens part of the economist's traditional theory of the firm. For the student of business, narrowly considered, there are the customary problems of control and administration. The sociologist turns to status, roles, and the informal structure, as well as to the microcosmos itself. Political scientists join several other groups in the interest in power and authority in hierarchical structures, and in the institutional forms of governing structures. Social psychologists apply their concepts about group structure and communication nets. In Bakke's "fusion processes" there are many of the variables related to the new union's problem of cohesiveness. There are both group processes and motivational issues in coalition formation, and information as a psychological variable becomes central to decision theory. It seems certain that this area will be one of the richest in generating both concepts and research in the near future.

In terms of the level of abstraction, the field is in a rather peculiar state. We have a group of relatively vigorous models of considerable formal elegance, on the one hand, from the mathematical economists and the decision theorists. On the other hand, we have some brilliant penetrating insights from the naturalistic observation of people like Whyte, Argyris, and Selznick. Between these, however, there is a remarkable gap.

We do not have much in the way of systematic behavioral data collected for the purpose of testing hypotheses or quantifying variables used in models. For example, we have models dealing with the cost of decentralized decision making in abstract terms, but we know nothing about the information and decision load that can be supported, or how individuals vary along this dimension. Again, classical economic theory has seen a limit on the size of the firm in the fact that there is only one top decision maker in an organization, while the supply is (virtually) infinite in the industry. But this principle has not been re-fined with work on the influence of delegation, rationalization of function, the nature of the information and decisions, and the like. We know little about the effect of various communication structures and practices on alternative forms of organizations and their cohesive-ness. We know little about the way the organization is seen by its members, or whether this can be varied advantageously in different structures. In this field particularly, we seem to have both the concepts (from several fields) and the methods. We should be just on the brink of a period of exciting systematic data collection.

The interest in the organization of large groups in industry has opened one area which seems to have particular promise for future development in the general psychological theory of motivation, and for a fruitful interaction between psychological and sociological approaches.

In motivational theory in general, and in its industrial applications in particular, motives have been largely dealt with as if there were tangible things present to different degrees in individuals. Following the instinct tradition, there has been a tendency to treat motives as residing within the individual, rather than as an interaction between the person and his environment. Several recent studies seem to be approaching a kind of geographical ecology of motivation at work. Walker and Guest (93) made a detailed interview study of workers on an assembly line. They found, for example, that the number of contacts a worker had with his fellows at work was not only related to his expressed satisfactions, but was also related to such company-relevant indices as turnover, grievances, and the amount of pay necessary to keep a man on the job. The assembly line almost necessarily is stretched out in a long thin line, and the very geography of production, originally designed with only technological merits in mind, is discovered to have liabilities in human performance. Similarly, in England, when technological advances made it profitable to mine thin coal seams by a "long wall" method, the strength of both small face-to-face groups and of the larger inclusive group was weakened, with an increase in accidents and a decrease in production. In the new system, instead of concentrating a small group at a seam-face to do a complete job of loosening, gathering, and transporting coal, a shift attacked a long seam, loosening coal for an entire period, after which another shift gathered and transported. This change so weakened the structure of the group (with loss to the company) that it was necessary to find other ways to rebuild the small group relations and the larger organization. When this was done, accidents went down and productivity went up (Trist and Bamforth, 88). Studies like these lead us to see the machine and machine-layout less as a tool for production than as a part of the topography of the individual's work place, and, as such, provide a way to study the geographical ecology of motivation. They seem surprisingly similar to the findings of the urban sociologists, as they investigate the change in social organization flowing from the change from the wheel-spoke towns of the railroad days to the modern strip-towns growing up along the highways. So far the two fields have not come together on the problem, but it seems profitable for them to do so. At the same time, it is worth noticing that such studies have implications for the human engineer's analysis of work-systems, and the geographical ecology of motivation adds another dimension to the human variables with which he should deal in the design of work for the optimum utilization of human characteristics.

Jaques' *Changing Culture of a Factory* (56) brings up the same kind of problem, though his basis of analysis is more topological than geographical. Similarly, some of the studies of rumor and communication demand a kind of a grid-system against which to see the group processes. Davis (34), in studying "grapevine" communication systems in industry, shows isolates in the network, both on the basis of geographical position and functional position in the group. Weiss and Jacobsen (97), using a very large sociometric matrix of communication contacts, similarly identified both isolates and liaison people within the group. In non-industrial studies of rumor transmission (Back, *et al.,* 7) both geographical and functional position assume importance in communication. Further study of the lay-out of the social group seems promising for such process analyses as well as for the ecology of motivation.

SMALL GROUPS

In the interest in smaller groups, two lines are evident: the structural, which might be seen flowing from Moreno's sociometry, and that of group dynamics, stemming from Lewin. The Lewinians raise the problem of group cohesiveness, though the problem has not proven particularly amenable to attack either theoretically or experimentally. They have focused considerable attention on group problem solving (Kelley and Thibault, 60) and group decision, and it is from the latter area that the biggest influence on industrial studies has come. Referring back frequently to Allport's article on participation (1), and, in the most detailed study of the group, drawing heavily on Lewin's notion of quasi-stationary equilibrium (Coch and French, 30), they have produced a group of instances in industry where participative group decision overcomes resistance to change. While there is considerable evidence that participation is effective, we have very little suggestion as to why it is. Somehow, this technique seems able to muster the forces which hold the group together, and which often are barriers to the group's action, and make them positive.

Historically, the interest in small groups was refocused by the Hawthorne studies' discovery of the effectiveness of the group in determining productivity. They began, in the best engineering tradition, by asking, "will the introduction of rest pauses reduce fatigue and monotony and hence increase output?" Later, in an outburst of serendipity, they say, "it was clear that two essentially different sorts of changes occurred . . . those changes introduced by the investigators in the form of experimental conditions . . . and a gradual change in the social interrelations among the operators themselves and between the operators and the supervisors. From the attempt to set the proper conditions for the experiment, there arose indirectly a change in human relations which came to be of great significance (Roethlisberger and Dickson, 74, pp. 58–59). The new interest in the group's power to facilitate or inhibit change stems from this point.

The field of resistance to change is an old one in industrial social psychology. In 1927 Angles (2) published a detailed study of it, Mathewson a book in 1931 (67), but its base in group processes was not clear until it was suggested in the Hawthorne studies and vigorously followed up by the Lewinians. Angles, for example, spoke both of the signs of restriction and of its causes. He identified the reduction in the variance of production figures as an indicator of restriction twenty years before Lewin's hypothesis of gradients of forces around levels of performance made it theoretically meaningful. Angles interprets restriction chiefly in terms of individual factors, speaking of such things as fear of rate cutting, physiological factors, satisfaction with present earnings, and the like. He does mention (Angles, 2, p. 250) that "the practice seems to rest primarily on a strong sense of courtesy to one's mate . . ." and later, "loyalty to one's work-mate is usually so strong that a higher position with better wages in the same factory is not desired if it would mean separation from one's set of neighbors and friends. This is more marked in women than in men. . . . The herd instinct seems to operate in inverse ratio to the skill required for the work, and thus it quite commonly overcomes natural acquisitiveness." Two things seem interesting in this early quote: one, the fact that the force associated with the relations among workers was identified as part of the restriction of output and resistance to change, though it was not emphasized, and, two, the fact that it was still permissible to speak in instinct terms; the more modern terminology of social motives and restraining forces had not yet taken over. We seem clearly to have progressed in the more modern statements. It is now possible to identify and manipulate some of the factors in the group. However, further work on group processes outside the industrial field should lead us to more precise determinations of the source and nature of the problem at work.

In the industrial situation, the area of restriction of output is a somewhat strange case in which the very phenomenon has changed, partly because of its recognition and study, and partly because of a change in the environment in which it operates. Where originally it seemed firmly grounded in group cohesiveness and social motives, it has become apparently a much more conscious tool of bargaining. While at all times there seemed to be an element of fear of rate change, and a protest against what were perceived as too high rates of work, more recently the restriction of output seems to be used as a deliberate tool preliminary to bargaining for something else. For example, in the building trades, the railway workers, and longshoremen, restriction of output has lead to fixed work schedules—either shorter work-weeks or schedules based on units of production, with over-time pay for what would be normal productivity before restriction. Although the overt behavioral signs may remain the same, the psychological context underlying them may have changed radically to a more conscious use of the group's power to gain a leverage in a bargaining situation.

The small group theorists have also markedly changed the interpretation of leadership. Particularly in the industrial setting, the traditional view of the leader in the past was of a charismatic individual possessing the trait of leadership. A great deal of research went, without much success, into attempts to identify these qualities of leadership in the interest of selection. The emphasis on the group and group processes lead to a description of the leader in the mold of The Admirable Crichton—a man who, in the particular situation, possessed the skills and abilities to provide means for the satisfactions of the needs of group members. We now speak of the "emergent" leader, we distinguish between "headship" and "leadership," and we use "buddy ratings" to identify leaders. The pendulum has swung a long ways to one side, and the reverse trend is already discernible in the assessment field, in a return to the search for the qualities of leadership within the individual instead of the group. However, even as the pendulum swings back, it is more group-oriented, and the variables tend to deal with relations with others rather than decisiveness, forcefulness, and determination. For industrial studies of leadership, the problem will surely have to be referred to the growing body of studies of organization theory. For example, as the size of the group increases, the simple ability to hold the group together becomes one of the most important problems, and, in many cases, a corporate entity seems to direct itself a large proportion of the time, with the leader's job being to keep it working as a unit, to keep information flowing through it, and to adjust the parts to one another. Again, as the study of group process progresses, particularly as it moves toward organization theory, the restatement of the problem of leadership seems a likely fruitful outcome.

In the tradition of the sociometric analysis of the internal structure of groups, there is a lively development. Danzig and Galanter (33) and Weiss and Jacobsen (97) have proposed sophisticated sociometric analyses of industrial groups and demonstrated their applicability empirically. The techniques are computationally cumbersome, but they are encouraging in the indication that it is possible to work with groups of at least two or three hundred, and that fruitful results come from such analyses. The first of these studies provides operational meaningfulness to the concepts of cohesiveness, social distance, and centrality, using the terms somewhat as Bavelas (14) did in dealing with communications nets. Developed further, this would mean that it was possible to define all the radii of an industrial group at a given point in time, and, hence, to describe the shape of the organization in a much more functional manner than in the traditional "family tree" organization chart. If it were possible thus to represent the shape of the organization it would allow us to do a kind of longitudinal study which has been so far unavailable to social psychologists. The anthropometric studies in the area of child development have been fruitful sources of understanding. A similar historical picture of the growth of social organizations would seem equally promising if the means of representing shape and structure at various stages becomes available. The Weiss and Jacobsen study points to another similar possibility. They identified sub-groups on the basis of the kinds of contacts which occurred—separated work groups, liaison people, and isolates. Of their group of 200, about 18% were tentatively identified as having a liaison function. Again, this kind of analysis could provide a measure for the growth of organizations with which we could see the rate of demand for liaison as the size increases. Such studies could give us insight into the stresses within the system arising as a result of growth.

Also in the sociometric tradition, although a long ways from the origin, would be studies like Cartwright and Harary's (25) use of graph theory to deal with symmetry and asymmetry in attitudes within the structure. French (43) uses a similar approach to deal with social power. Such sociometric analyses have been urged as a management tool, or, as the sociometrist develops toward the study of interaction process, as a predictive device (Chapple, 28). The study of group structure through interaction process analysis has developed both in technique and theoretical statement (Bales, Flood, and Householder, 11). It is still cumbersome, but in some ways it is the natural bridge between the static structuralism of the pure sociometric tradition and the dynamics of the Lewinians.

A special variety of the study of interaction structures within groups is the field of communication nets and their relative effectiveness. Most of the work stems originally from Bavelas' model (14) and there has been a certain amount of sameness in both the form and findings of the empirical research (Bavelas, 15; Heise and Miller, 50; Leavitt, 63; Leavitt and Mueller, 63; Shaw, 80; Shaw and Rothschild, 81). The general pattern of this work has been the experimental manipulation of group structure and the measurement of performance and satisfaction. For example, groups may be organized in wheel or spoke fashion:

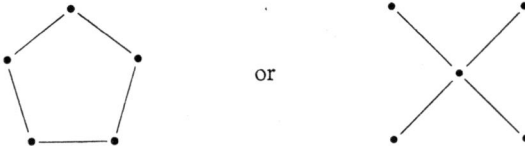

or

Communication may be restricted in direction or not:

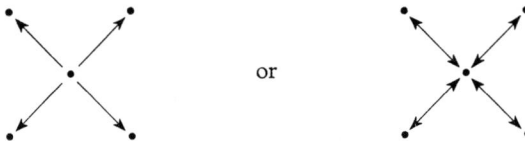

or

The major independent variables become the structure of the group in terms of communication channels, the centrality (i.e., distance from neighbors) of members, feedback, and type of task. The major dependent variables are accuracy of performance, satisfaction of members, and the location of the leader. In general, it is impossible to maximize productivity and satisfaction simultaneously. Highly centralized leadership works against rapid solutions. Increased feedback increases accuracy. High centrality for the whole group facilitates behavior. However, in view of the central role of communication and communications nets in the viability of industrial organizations, this must be seen as a point from which research progress will flow.

One other area of small group problems seems particularly relevant to economic behavior, although it is not possible to point to any considerable body of published work at present. Economic theory has always made hypotheses about both human motivation and interactions between people. Recent developments, following historically, though not necessarily logically, from the theory of games, contain two possibilities especially relevant for small group theory and research: utility curves for shared risk, and variable information in strategic decision matrices. It is not possible to do more than point to the existence of the problems here. It is possible to construct psychological curves (rather than strictly logical) for the risk an individual will run to gain a given objective. Such a function contains a multitude of factors, expectations, risk-taking proclivities, present position, and the like. The empirical curve is typically not monotonic. Such risks can be experimentally shared, in the fashion of pooled insurance risks, but it is not necessarily true that the new value will fall at the point indicated by dividing the risk and return by the number of sharers. The field suggests possibilities for a joint study of group structure and process and the economic area of risk-taking. On the other hand, strategic decision theory tends to rely on complete information or complete lack of it among participants in competitive situations; a situation which facilitates model building but does not approximate reality very closely. Again, it seems possible to bring to bear the techniques of the communication-net research and the work on cohesiveness in groups to add a realistic dimension to empirical studies of strategic decisions.

MOTIVATION

In many ways the history of the attempt to deal with motivation in industrial social psychology covers a large part of the whole field. Selection devices in the strict tradition of individual differences were soon seen to be inadequate on the simple level of skills and ability. Motivations were introduced here as individual variables in interest inventories like the Strong and Kuder. As the individual came to be studied in the context of the industrial organization, stress was put on higher order needs—for example, loss of social need satisfaction on the one hand through mishandling of group structure, and of egoistic need satisfaction on the other through de-skilling in the rationalization of jobs. Surveys of attitudes moved the motivational interest from the level of the individual to the group average. Questions were still asked individually, but the results, in terms of both the responses and the criterion (usually production), were from the total group. With somewhat discouraging results in a simple relationship between attitudes and criterial performance, interest shifted to studies of attitude change, and the "human relations" movement is largely a program of development of attitudes among leaders to manipulate the "climate" seen as a variable in early group studies. Finally, it is largely the interest in motivation that shapes psychological studies of organization, perhaps stemming from the early Lewinian suggestion that it is easier to reorganize the structure of the whole group than to change the individual and leave the group as it was. Within this sketchy overview lies a large proportion of the researches in industrial social psychology, a tremendous body of relatively unfruitful work on attitudes, and some promises for future progress.

In general, the studies of attitudes and productivity stem from the law of effect notion in learning theory: organisms tend to seek out situations that are rewarding and avoid those that are punishing. Katz and Kahn (58) make this explicit for human relations, Haire (49) for industrial leadership, and Brayfield and Crockett (18) for attitude studies. E. L. Thorndike's original formulation said, substantially, that if a modifiable connection between a stimulus and a response is followed by a satisfying state of affairs the connection between stimulus and response will be strengthened. Restated, if the response of high productivity may or may not follow the stimulus of the work situation, a generally satisfying state accompanying it will increase the probability that the response will occur. Even at this simple level, there are some problems. One, this principle guarantees nothing about the emergence of high productivity as a response; it only refers to strengthening the tendency for it to re-appear. Two, to be effective, it demands control over the satisfying state. When high productivity appears the satisfaction must follow; when low productivity occurs it must be withheld. Even if this were possible, its practical wisdom as a course is open to question. Finally, for those cases where low productivity is accompanied by satisfactions related to some other source, there is very little to be done.

As a theory of learning, this principle has been challenged. It has been suggested that the satisfaction must reduce the drive that elicited the original behavior. There must be a relationship between the productivity and the satisfaction. Now the problem becomes very difficult in practice. Even if rewards can uniformly be provided for productivity, other drives—for socialization with others, for defying the boss (autonomy?)—will find drive-reducing rewards in any but the most austere situation. In general, the abstract principle is clear. The coordinating definitions which tie it to productivity, however, leave real doubt about its operation, and, indeed, a summary of a host of empirical investigations would suggest that a positive relation between the two is tenuous at best. On the positive side, the law of effect would involve the worker finding satisfactions on the job, and these would be revealed by appropriate attitude surveys. It is not necessarily true, however, that the pursuit of these satisfactions would lead to productivity. On the negative side, lack of satisfactions might be expected to lead to avoidance of the job-situation, and, since presence is a necessary condition for productivity, to reduced criterial performance. Indeed, some studies do suggest a relation between negative attitudes and withdrawal in the form of turnover, accidents, and absenteeism (Brayfield and Crockett, 18). On the positive side, however, we seem to need considerably more differentiation of motivational theory to serve as an intervening variable between surveyed attitudes and observed productivity, and better coordinating definition between the motivational constructs and the realities of the industrial situation.

A step in this direction is occurring in motivational analyses. The Michigan studies of productivity and morale (Katz, Maccoby, Gurin, and Floor, 59), for example, introduce intervening steps of group-oriented versus task-oriented supervision between the attitude and the criterion. Without this kind of differentiation, the methodological elegance of scaling and the development of sub-scales in attitude surveys seems likely to be of little use in the future on this problem, as it has been in the past. The studies of Walker and Guest, referred to above, broke attitudes down into social satisfactions associated with contacts on the job, egoistic satisfactions associated with feeling of achievement at work, and the like. While these studies did not relate the findings to criterial performance, they provide a step toward it. Similarly, a group of other studies (Katz and Kahn, 58; Schaffer, 76; Wickert, 99) suggest the possibility of identifying and producing egoistic satisfactions at work, and, in some cases, of relating them to criterial performance.

The assumption that high levels of satisfaction of the individual's needs will be related to productivity does not seem to hold. Put in these terms it is not surprising; there is no reason to believe that the individual's goals and the organization's will coincide. A more detailed understanding of the kinds of satisfactions determining behavior at work (productive and other) and, particularly, the ecology of drives at work suggested above would seem to be needed before simple relationships between morale and productivity can be hoped for.

As has been pointed out before, it was very much the vogue at one time to attack the motivational concept of the economic man. For example, it has been said, the piece rates incentive is based on faulty assumptions both of kind and amount. The single motive involved (money) does not do justice to the complexities of human drive systems. In amount, such a reward plan unnecessarily makes a simple unwarranted assumption of "more reward—more performance." While the objection to the single motive and the monotonic function seems sound, we might notice that the same form is repeated in many modern notions. It is quite clear in the case of participation. We have some experimental evidence that participation improves performance. Beyond that, however, it certainly seems to be suggested that more reward will produce more performance. This is an extension that is wholly unjustified and unsupported. It is not explicitly suggested that participation alone is the motive, but it receives a remarkable preponderance of attention. Somewhat the same assumption seems to be made in several areas: if communication is good, more communication is better. If decentralization and delegation is good, more is better. It seems clear that there are two steps in this argument. Factor A must be shown to be effective. Then an increase in factor A must be shown to produce an increment in the dependent variable. It may or may not be necessary to go on to identify the shape of the function of increase. In this connection, the Law of Effect (which underlies most of this reasoning) suggests that the probability of a response will be increased by reward. It does not necessarily involve the proposition that an increase in reward will increase the probability still more.

One area of motivational studies is surprisingly lacking —the study of the motivation of management. While psychologists have inveighed vigorously against the oversimplifications of the Economic Man as a motivational model for workers, I suspect that we have largely kept it in interpreting management behavior. The manager is seen generally as actuated by money and power as motives, almost as if there were a difference in kind between superiors and subordinates. A broad program of investigation in this area would seem worthwhile; it would also tie in well with the assessment approaches to the identification of high level talent. As it develops, such an interest would go beyond the simple motivational interpretation of behavior, and, perhaps, lead us to a statement of what might be called a philosophy of management. Now, when the corporation is taking on a very different role in the national social structure, and when the professional manager is a dominant figure in the corporation, the general value systems in which he operates become of especial importance. The other side of this coin, in a sense, is the social role of the manager. The American manager has a quite different role in the view of the public from the position of the manager in most of the other Western countries. Indeed, much of the strength of American industry seems to flow from this. It would seem an appropriate area for study to investigate this closely. Such work would be closely related to the companion studies of role perceptions of managers of themselves and of their positions, and of the influence of hierarchical levels on self-perception.

It seems somewhat strange that the motivational analysis has not included the various levels of management. Studies of fatigue have concentrated on the worker, whose hours are typically much less than the manager. The emphasis on social and egoistic need satisfactions at work have been primarily on the hourly paid worker, as if he alone had the sensibilities to avoid the rigid determinism of economic motivation. Some of the role problems of the foreman in complex structures have been pointed to (Ghiselli and Lodahl, 44; Porter, in press), though there is little research, but there is virtually no work in psychology on prestige and status as springs of action in the management structure. Our picture of the problems of human motivation and organizational goals will never be complete without an analysis of the directing part of the structure as well as the larger portion of the work force.

COMMUNICATION

The general problem of communications has long been a part of industrial psychology. Early it was largely stimulus bound. The human engineering work on the size of type is in this tradition, and, to a large extent, the Flesch count is a modernization of this original question, substituting length of sentences for size of type. Early work in advertising, too, generally followed this tradition, concentrating on stimulus characteristics designed to attract attention. On the side of the criterion, early studies were equally simple, concentrating on a simple undifferentiated "yes-no" criterion of comprehension, recognition, or recall. In advertising, for example, recall may be a *sine qua non* to effectiveness. It is possible, but perhaps unlikely, for a display to have an effect if it can not be recalled. However the fruitful part of the problem seems to be beyond this. How is the fact integrated into cognitive structures? With what motivational systems does it make contact? These and similar problems become the proper study of communication in general. More recently, work on communication has turned to structural factors in groups, mentioned above, and to a more detailed study of the process of communication.

As the problem moves from the simple one of stimulus presentation and a criterion of recall or failure to recall, the details of the process become important. In industry itself, some studies have suggested that certain kinds of information can be differentially utilized by workers (Chisholm, 29). Hovland and co-workers (Hovland, 53; Hovland, Janis, and Kelley, 54) have considerably differentiated and enlarged the stimulus problem. They raise the problem of primacy, tying the problem of mediating attitude change to more traditional learning studies. They also extend earlier work on the prestige of the communicator by varying source credibility, and open the subject's motivational system by studying the effects of fear-arousing propaganda. The Yale studies also enlarged the criterion problem, studying the process as well as the fact of retention by observing changes in material over a period of time. Further internalization of the process is indicated by the suggestion that specific steps of identification, internalization, and compliance can fruitfully be recognized in the subject. Cartwright (24) made some detailed suggestions about the conditions necessary for communication to produce a change in attitude. Another facet of the process has been opened by Festinger's inquiry into the motives for communication (39). Most of these developments have been in relatively pure laboratory situations rather than in industry. However, the variables seem immediately relevant to present industrial problems, and the progress in stating the problem promises future growth in the attack on communication in industry.

The rise in the field of social perception probably deserves to be included under the general heading of communication, since it deals with variables influencing the reception of stimulus information. The term "social perception" seems to have two distinct meanings (apart from the third usage which Brunswik gave it): on the one hand, the influence of the social group on the process of perception, stemming from the Sherif experiments on autokinetic movement, of which the conformity studies already mentioned are ideological descendants. The other meaning is the perception of social phenomena—of personalities, roles, institutions, and the like. Here there is a great deal of work relevant to industrial problems—studies of roles and role perceptions in hierarchies, of labor and management's perceptions of one another, of the personality or corporate image of the firm and the definition of leadership in terms of the perception of superiors and subordinates.

In dealing with the problem of information presentation under the general heading of human engineering, it was necessary to broaden the problem somewhat to the problem of decision theory, the requirements of information in teams, and information under conditions of uncertainty. Somewhat the same set of problems appear properly under the present heading. Edwards (38) summarized the work on decision making and its relation to economic behavior, and the field has made some progress since that time. It still seems an unusually fruitful area for research. Atkinson, for example, (6) has opened the question of motivational determinants of risk-taking behavior, and Scodal and others (Scodal, Ratoosh, and Minas, 77), returning to the tradition of the personnel psychologist, have investigated the personality correlates of risk-taking. The questions in this area are directly related to the typical business situation, and make it possible to bring psychological principles to bear most immediately. It has been pointed out before that the psychologist has traditionally inveighed against an oversimplified concept of economic man as a model for motivation. The risk-taking problem lets us test more sophisticated motivational notions directly in the very situation for which the economic man model was invented. Expectations, levels of aspiration, past experience, and self concepts all are relevant to the risk-taker's behavior. The amount and kind of information is a variable in strategic decision matrices. The position of an individual within a group bears an immediate relevance to the problem. In a sense the restriction of output already referred to is part of the problem — either in its original sense of turning away from economic advantage to maximize social need satisfactions, illustrating some transitivity in motivational values in utility curves, or in its more recent sense of a more complex bargaining for contractual advantages in a situation more nearly approaching the classic theory of games. The combination of these problems with, for example, those of the experimental sharing of risks, and the human engineer's interest in information display, would seem to indicate a broad and fruitful field for the future.

Summary

A summary should do two things: 1) show the threads of psychological thinking in the field, 2) illustrate the common problems and research areas of joint behavioral sciences. Consequently the following brief statement is divided into two parts.

PSYCHOLOGICAL THREADS

1 The history of the field points to the term "psychology in industry," rather than "industrial psychology." Within it three quite separate traditions thrive: the experimentalist, manipulating an independent variable which is usually a physical stimulus, the differential psychologist, and the social psychologist. Each of the three carries the threads of general psychological theory, and the development of the field is primarily the development of psychology, modified somewhat by external societal pressures, and somewhat less by specific demands of industrial problems.

2 In general, the whole field has focused on work, workers, and the conditions of work, and, to some extent, in spite of the interest in leadership, neglected the problems of the motivation of management, conditions of work for leaders, and the like. Recent interest in the general problem of organization seems to draw attention to the over-all problem of the operation rather than the level of production.

3 Traditional personnel psychology seems to have stalled on the problem of selection and classification, though iterative solutions to the classification problem provide a new elegance. The problem of the criterion continues to be the chief stumbling block, as it has been for forty years. Assessment of high level talent and research on creativity is opening a new route in this area, with the possibility of taking advantage of the arithmetic of correlation to provide considerably greater leverage in the selection of men for managerial positions. Like the criterion problem, the assessment of training continues to be much discussed and little dealt with.

4 Among the areas which look promising for the future, that combining the problems of risk-taking and decision theory seems to take in most of the psychological fields and to promise relatively immediate yields. Outside of psychology there is a good deal of theoretical development to set the problem. Within psychology, most of the fields concerned bear on it. The differential psychologist concerns himself

with personality correlates of risk-taking, the engineer with information in decision making, and the social theorist with motivational problems in both areas and with the structure of groups, for example, in shared risks. Relatively few publications have appeared in this area, so far.

5 A second area which combines the various fields is the growing interest in organization theory. The communications theorist approaches it through the problem of networks, the human engineer approaches it through a similar problem in providing information in complex systems, and the social psychologist enters the problem through the various routes of motivation, group structure, and roles and status. There is considerable activity in the field, but a surprising dearth of empirical research. Though we have quite a few theoretical statements about how organizations grow, we have, surprisingly, virtually no simple histories of how they have in fact grown. Both empirical and theoretical work in this area seems just around the corner.

6 Running through a good many problems, one development seems associated with progress, as it is in psychology in general. Where a new advance has been made, it has usually been with a differentiation of the criterion of the original problem, which made it possible to bring to bear other areas of psychological theory. For example, in communication, the advance from an early stimulus bound tradition is marked by the work of Hovland and his co-workers in opening problems of recall and long-term effect on the one hand, and conditions of the communicated material on the other. Festinger opened the question of motivation for communication, and the psychological process became the topic rather than the simple fact of communication. Again, in the area of selection, where the criterion seems to block further research, a simple lengthening in time of the criterion measure might lead the way to further insight. Present criteria are usually relatively shortly after employment, and obscure the nature of the development of criterion performance. Longer measures might lead to attention to the slope of the curve of response to training, to the interaction of treatment and aptitudes, or to the change in factorial content of skills with practice. In the general area of work and productivity,

the Coch and French study of resistance to change shows the benefit from differentiation of the criterion and the provision of theoretical meaningfulness to the new parts. Similarly, in the studies of motivation and production, the opening of the area of the ecology of motivation by studying the workplace both advances the understanding and broadens the theoretical base on which it rests. If there is one touchstone to advance in these problems, the progressive differentiation of the criterion would seem to be it.

7 Finally, a group of other problems seem to have the support in psychological theory for development in this field. The problems of roles and status in well organized hierarchies, the general area of a shifting management philosophy in response to changes in the corporation and the society, and the problem of conformity are illustrative. In some cases the psychological problem needs to be broadened to include the societal one, as for example, in the selection area. As technology demands more and more high level skills, we tend to try to identify and assign them as if we were drawing from a bottomless pool. We treat special aptitudes much the way we once treated the buffalo or the forest problem, giving little thought to the fact that in each case we are exhausting a finite population. As we build more technical schools, staff more laboratories, and rationalize more industrial operations, we will need careful demographic studies of the available skills and an attack on the classification problem on a broad scale to maximize the utilization of skills, not within an operation but over a wide group of them. It is not at all suggested that research on psychological problems in industry should be largely guided by pressures outside the field. Past advance on the contrary basis is too persuasive an argument for that. However, the very success in applying psychological principles to the problems in business and industry forces us to broaden the base of our interest to include, to some extent, the developments both within the industrial complex and in the society in which it is imbedded.

JOINT PROBLEMS

1 Some joint problems have already been referred to. Certain of them demand the conceptual frameworks of both fields. For example,

the area of shared risks needs both the economic notion of utility and the psychological approach to group structure. Team theory generates demands for estimates of the loading in certain kinds of performance which can be borne by members. Organization theory clearly flows from both disciplines.

2. Certain areas of business administration seem to rest specifically on psychological concepts. For example, pay plans are partly built on notions about motivation—both about kinds of motives and their gradients of growth. Similarly, the treatment of seniority rests on a base of assumption about the use of reward and its effect on behavior. The problem of satisfaction and the general area of human relations dealt with here, would be in this class.

3. Some problems seem to depend on simple technological contribution from well developed areas of psychology. Selection and classification, or the design of equipment are good examples of this type.

4 A large group of problems remain where joint effort seems most appropriate. In the area of social perception, for example, we have barely opened the field of role perceptions in hierarchical structures. Some work has been done on the perception of one level by another, and it looks promising. Some exists in self-perceptions characteristic of different levels, and, likewise, it should develop. We have virtually nothing of what has been called "psychological job descriptions" (45). That is, descriptions of the aspects of the job which, besides simple duties, make demands on the person—the fact, for example, that a waitress is caught between the customer's demands and the kitchen's inflexibility. Such phenomena, at different levels, have all sorts of costs to the organization, from higher pay scales, turnover and absenteeism, to ulcers and coronary pathology in executives.

In the labor-management field, the problem of dual allegiances seems to have important cognitive and motivational implications for practice. Role perceptions (and misperceptions) of one another in bargaining relationships have been studied. In one case, in a rare example, a careful study of the behavioral effects of arbitration has been done (75). This is an unusually good case in which the policies and practices from business can be investigated in the tradition of the behavioral sciences. Ross asks the question "what was the effect (as shown by behavior) of reinstatement by arbitration?" Similar studies seem appropriate on the Law of Effect. Presumably disciplinary punishments are handed out on the assumption that the behavior will be modified. In general societal behavior, the determinants and criteria are too complex to make study easy. Here, the criteria of good behavior are explicit and available, the population is relatively stable, and the opportunity to test hypotheses seems endless.

In the area of management behavior, also, there seems to be a rich field. We need simple studies of what happens like Sune Carlson's study (22) of Swedish executives. The studies of decision go beyond these. The motivation of management has been very little investigated—though some attention has been given to compensation plans under high tax rates. Job descriptions of management are inadequate, but our knowledge of the perceptions of members of management of their jobs is even more so.

In general, the time seems ripe for a joint effort of students of business administration and the ancillary behavioral disciplines, bringing concepts and methods from a variety of fields to bear on a set of common problems.

References

1. ALLPORT, G. W. "The Psychology of Participation," *Psychological Review*, 1945, 53, 117–32.
2. ANGLES, A. "Restriction of Output," *Journal of the National Institute of Industrial Psychology*, 1927, 3, 248–51.
3. ARENSBERG, C. M., and D. McGREGOR. "Determination of Morale in an Industrial Company," *Journal of Applied Anthropology*, 1942, 1, 12–34.
4. ARGYRIS, C. *Personality and Organization.* New York, Harper and Bros., 1957.
5. ASCH, S. E. "Studies of Independence and Conformity," *Psychological Monographs*, 1956, 70 (9), (Whole No. 416).
6. ATKINSON, J. W. "Motivational Determinants of Risk-taking Behavior," *Psychological Review*, 1957, 64, 359–72.
7. BACK, K., L. FESTINGER, B. HYMOVITCH, H. KELLEY, S. SCHACTER, and J. THIBAULT. "The Methodology of Studying Rumour Transmission," *Human Relations*, 1950, 3, 307–312.

8. BAKKE, E. W. *The Bonds of Organization.* New York, Harper and Bros., 1950.

9. BAKKE, E. W. *The Fusion Process.* New Haven, Conn., Yale University, Labor and Management Center, 1953.

10. BAKKE, E. W., and C. ARGYRIS. *Organization Structure and Dynamics: A Framework for Theory.* New Haven, Conn., Yale University, Labor and Management Center, 1954.

11. BALES, R. F., M. FLOOD, and A. S. HOUSEHOLDER. *Some Group Interaction Models.* USAF Project Rand, Research Memorandum 953, 1952.

12. BARNARD, C. I. "Functions and pathology of status systems in formal organizations." In W. F. WHYTE (ed.). *Industry and Society.* New York, McGraw-Hill Book Co., 1946.

13. BARNARD, C. I. *The Functions of the Executive.* Cambridge, Mass., Harvard University Press, 1950.

14. BAVELAS, A. "A Mathematical Model for Group Structures," *Applied Anthropology,* 1948, 7, 16–30.

15. BAVELAS, A. "Communication Patterns in Task-oriented Groups," *Journal of the Acoustical Society of America,* 1950, 22, 725–30.

16. BAXTER, B., A. A. TAAFFE, and J. HUGHES. "A Training Evaluation Study," *Personnel Psychology,* 1953, 6, 403–417.

17. BIRMINGHAM, H. P., and F. V. TAYLOR. "A Design Philosophy for Man-machine Control Systems," *Proceedings of the Institute of Radio Engineers,* New York, 1954, 42, 1748–58.

18. BRAYFIELD, A. H., and W. H. CROCKETT. "Employee Attitudes and Employee Performance," *Psychological Bulletin,* 1955, 52, 396–424.

19. BROWN, C. W., and E. E. GHISELLI. "Per Cent Increase in Proficiency Resulting from Use of Selective Devices," *Journal of Applied Psychology,* 1953, 37, 341–44.

20. BROWN, J. S., and W. O. JENKINS. "An Analysis of Human Motor Abilities Related to the Design of Equipment and a Suggested Plan of Research." In P. M. FITTS (ed.). *Psychological Research on Equipment Design.* Report No. 19, AAF, Aviation Psychology Program Research Reports. Washington, D. C., U. S. Government Printing Office, 1947.

21. BUCHELE, R. B. "Company Character and the Effectiveness of Personnel Management," *Personnel,* 1955, 31, 289–302.

22. CARLSON, SUNE. *Executive Behavior.* Strombergs, Stockholm, 1951.

23. CARTER, C. F., G. P. MEREDITH, and G. L. S. SHAKLE (eds.). *Uncertainty and Business Decisions.* Liverpool, The University Press, 1954.

24. CARTWRIGHT, D. "Some Principles of Mass Persuasion," *Human Relations,* 1949, 2, 253–425.

25. CARTWRIGHT, D., and F. HARARY. "Structural Balance: A Generalization of Heider's Theory," *Psychological Review*, 1956, 63, 277–93.

26. CHAPANIS, A. "Applied Experimental Psychology," *Personnel Psychology*, 1952, 5, 46–48.

27. CHAPANIS, A., W. GARNER, and C. MORGAN. *Applied Experimental Psychology*. New York, John Wiley and Sons, 1949.

28. CHAPPLE, E. D. "The Standard Experimental (Stress) Interview as Used in Interaction Chronograph Investigations," *Human Organization*, 1953, 12, 21–37.

29. CHISHOLM, C. (ed.). *Communication in Industry*. London, Business Publ. Ltd., 1955.

30. COCH, L., and J. R. P. FRENCH. "Overcoming Resistance to Change," *Human Relations*, 1948, 1, 512–32.

31. GRONBACH, L. J. "The Two Disciplines of Scientific Psychology," *American Psychologist*, 1957, 12, 671–85.

32. CRUTCHFIELD, R. "Conformity and Character," *American Psychologist*, 1955, 10, 191–98.

33. DANZIG, E. R., and E. H. GALANTER. *The dynamics and structure of small industrial work groups*. Series 1955, Report No. 7, Institute for Research on Human Relations, Philadelphia, Pa.

34. DAVIS, K. "Management Communication and the Grapevine," *Harvard Business Review*, 1953, 31, 43–49.

35. DENNIS, W. (ed.). *Current Trends in Industrial Psychology*. Pittsburgh, Pa., University of Pittsburgh Press, 1949.

36. DRUCKER, P. *America's Next Twenty Years*. New York, Harper and Bros., 1955.

37. EDGERTON, H. A. "Some Needs in Training Research," *Personnel Psychology*, 1955, 8, 19–25.

38. EDWARDS, W. "The Theory of Decision Making," *Psychological Bulletin*, 1954, 51, 380–418.

39. FESTINGER, L. "Informal Social Communication," *Psychological Review*, 1950, 57, 271–82.

40. FITTS, P. M. "Engineering Psychology and Equipment Design." In S. S. STEVENS (ed.). *Handbook of Experimental Psychology*. New York, John Wiley and Sons, 1951.

41. FLEISHMAN, E. A. "Leadership Climate, Human Relations Training, and Supervisory Behavior," *Personnel Psychology*, 1953, 6, 205–222.

42. FLEISHMAN, E. A., and W. E. HEMPEL, JR. "Changes in Factor Structure of a Complex Psychomotor Test as a Function of Practice," *Psychometrika*, 1954, 19, 239–52.

43. FRENCH, J. R. P. "A Formal Theory of Social Power," *Psychological Review,* 1956, 63, 181–94.
44. GHISELLI, E. E., and T. M. LODAHL. "The Evaluation of Foremen's Performance in Relation to the Internal Characteristics of Their Work Groups," *Personnel Psychology,* 1958, 11, 179–87.
45. HAIRE, M. "Industrial Social Psychology." In G. LINDZEY (ed.). *Handbook of Social Psychology.* Cambridge, Mass., Addison-Wesley, 1954.
46. HAIRE, M. "Role Perceptions in Labor-Management Relations: An Experimental Approach," *Industrial and Labor Relations Review,* VIII, 1955, 204–216.
47. HAIRE, M. "Size, Shape, and Function in Industrial Organizations," *Human Organization,* 1955, 14, 17–22.
48. HAIRE, M. "Interpersonal Relations in Collective Bargaining," In C. M. ARENSBERG, S. BARKIN, W. E. CHALMERS, H. WILENSKY, J. WORTHY, and BARBARA DENNIS (eds.). *Research in Industrial Human Relations.* New York, Harper and Bros., 1957.
49. HAIRE, M. *Psychology in Management.* New York, McGraw-Hill Book Co., 1957.
50. HEISE, G., and G. MILLER. "Problem Solving by Small Groups Using Various Communication Nets," *Journal of Abnormal and Social Psychology,* 1951, 46, 327–35.
51. HELMER, O. "The Game-Theoretical Approach to Organization Theory," *Rand Corporation Research Reports, P-1026.* Santa Monica, Calif., Feb. 19, 1957.
52. HERBST, P. G. "Measurement of Behavior Structure by Means of Input-Output Data," *Human Relations,* 1957, X, 4, 335–347.
53. HOVLAND, C. I. *The Order of Presentation in Persuasion.* New Haven, Conn., Yale University Press, 1957.
54. HOVLAND, C. I., I. L. JANIS, and H. H. KELLEY. *Communication and Persuasion.* New Haven, Conn., Yale University Press, 1953.
55. HULL, C. L. *Aptitude testing.* New York, World Book Co., 1928.
56. JAQUES, E. *The Changing Culture of a Factory.* New York, Dryden Press, 1952.
57. JENNINGS, E. E. "Democratic Supervision Thrives Only in the Right Group Climate," *Personnel,* 1955, 33, 296–99.
58. KATZ, D., and R. L. KAHN. "Some Recent Findings in Human-Relations Research in Industry." In SWANSON, NEWCOMB, and HARTLEY (eds.). *Readings in Social Psychology.* New York, Henry Holt and Co., 1952.
59. KATZ, D., N. MACCOBY, G. GURIN, and L. G. FLOOR. *Productivity, Supervision, and Morale Among Railroad Workers.* Ann Arbor, Mich., University of Michigan Press, 1951.
60. KELLEY, H., and J. THIBAULT. "Group Problem Solving." In GARDNER and

LINDZEY (eds.). *Handbook of Social Psychology*. Cambridge, Mass., Addison Wesley, 1955.

61. KORNHAUSER, A., and A. SHARP. "Employee Attitudes: Suggestions From a Study in a Factory," *Personnel Journal*, 1932, 10, 393–401.

62. LEAVITT, H. J. "Some Effects of Certain Communication Patterns on Group Performance," *Journal of Abnormal and Social Psychology*, 1951, 46, 38–40.

63. LEAVITT, H. J., and R. MUELLER. "Some Effects of Feedback on Communication," *Human Relations*, 1951, 4, 401–410.

64. MAIER, N. R. F. "An Experimental Test of the Effect of Training on Discussion Leadership," *Human Relations*, 1953, 6, 161–73.

65. MAIER, N. R. F. *Psychology in Industry*. New York, Houghton Mifflin Co., 1955.

66. MARSCHAK, J. "On Optimal Communication Rules for Teams," *Cowles Commission Discussion Paper, Economics No. 2029*. New Haven, Conn., Yale University, Jan. 29, 1952.

67. MATHEWSON, S. B. *Restriction of Output Among Unorganized Workers*. New York, Viking Press, 1931.

68. McGEHEE, W., and D. H. LIVINGSTON. "Persistence of the Effects of Training Employees to Reduce Waste," *Personnel Psychology*, 1954, 7, 33–39.

69. McGREGOR, D. M. "Conditions of Effective Leadership in the Industrial Organization," *Journal of Consulting Psychology*, 1944, 8, 55–63.

70. McGREGOR, D. "The Staff Function in Human Relations," *Journal of Social Issues*, IV, 3, 1948, 6–23.

71. MILLS, C. W. *White Collar*. New York, Oxford University Press, 1956.

72. PORTER, L. W. "Self-Perceptions of First-Level Supervisors Compared With Upper-Management Personnel and With Operative Line Workers," *Journal of Applied Psychology* (in press).

73. RADNER, R. "On Optimal Communications Rules for Certain Types of Teams," *Cowles commission discussion paper, Economics, No. 2064*. New Haven, Conn., Yale University, Jan. 8, 1953.

74. ROETHLISBERGER, F., and W. J. DICKSON. *Management and the Worker*. Cambridge, Mass., Harvard University Press, 1939.

75. ROSS, A. M. "The Arbitration of Discharge Cases: What Happens After Reinstatement," in *Critical Issues in Labor Arbitration*. Bureau of National Affairs, Washington, 1957.

76. SCHAFFER, R. "Job satisfaction as related to need satisfaction at work," *Psychological Monographs*, 1953, 67 (14) no. 364.

77. SCODAL, A., P. RATOOSH, and J. S. MINAS. "Some Personality Correlates of Decision Making Under Conditions of Risk," *Behavioral Sciences* (in press).

78. SELZNICK, P. *Leadership and Administration*. New York, Row, Peterson and Co., 1958.

79. SHARTLE, C. L. "Organization structure." In W. DENNIS (ed.). *Current Trends in Industrial Psychology*. Pittsburgh, Pa., University of Pittsburgh Press, 1949.

80. SHAW, M. E. "A Comparison of Two Types of Leadership in Various Communication Nets," *Journal of Abnormal and Social Psychology*, 1955, 50, 127–34.

81. SHAW, M. E., and G. H. ROTHSCHILD. "Some Effects of Prolonged Experience in Communication Nets," *Journal of Applied Psychology*, 1956, 40, 281–86.

82. SIMON, H. A. "A Comparison of Organization Theories," *Review of Economic Studies*, 1952, 20, 40–48.

83. SIMON, H. A. "Comments on the Theory of Organizations," *American Political Science Review*, 1952, 46, 1130–39.

84. SIMON, H. A. *Administrative Behavior*. New York, The Macmillan Co., 1955.

85. STAGNER, R. *The Psychology of Industrial Conflict*. New York, John Wiley and Sons, 1957.

86. TEAD, O. *Instincts in Industry*. New York, McGraw-Hill Book Co., 1918.

87. THORNDIKE, R. L. *Personnel Selection, Test and Measurement Techniques*. New York, John Wiley and Sons, 1949.

88. TRIST, E. L., and V. BAMFORTH. "Some Social and Psychological Consequences of the Longwall Method of Coal-Getting," *Human Relations*, 1951, 4, 3–38.

89. TUDDENHAM, R. "The Influence of a Group Norm on Individual Performance," *Journal of Psychology*, 1958, 46, 227–41.

90. U. S. NAVY SPECIAL DEVICES CENTER. *Bibliography of Human Engineering Reports*. (Unclassified). Fort Washington, N. Y., USN Special Devices Center, 1955, 13 pp.

91. VEBLEN, T. *The Instinct of Workmanship*. New York, Viking Press, 1918.

92. VITELES, M. S. *Motivation and Morale in Industry*. New York, W. W. Norton and Co., 1953.

93. WALKER, C. R., and R. H. GUEST. *The Man on the Assembly Line*. Cambridge, Mass., Harvard University Press, 1952.

94. WALLACE, S. R., JR., and C. M. TWITCHELL. "An Evaluation of a Training Course for Life Insurance Agents," *Personnel Psychology*, 1953, 6, 25–43.

95. WALLACE, S. R., JR., and J. WEITZ. "Industrial Psychology," in *Annual Review of Psychology*, 1955, 6, 217–50.

96. WEISS, R. S. "A Structure-Function Approach to Organization," *Journal of Social Issues*, 1956, 12, 61–67.

97. WEISS, R. S., and E. JACOBSEN. "A Method for the Analysis of the Structure of Complex Organizations," *American Sociological Review*, 1955, 20, 661–68.

98. WHYTE, W. H., JR. *The Organization Man*. New York, Doubleday and Co., 1956.

99. WICKERT, F. "Turnover and Employee's Feelings of Ego-Involvement in the Day-to-Day Operations of a Company," *Personnel Psychology,* 1951, 4, 185–97.

100. WILLIAMS, W. *Mainsprings of Man*. New York, Charles Scribner's Sons, 1925.

BY PAUL F. LAZARSFELD

Sociological Reflections

on Business:

Consumers and Managers

We can take it for granted that a majority of the sociologists teaching in American liberal arts colleges will have an ideological bias against business. Aiding the doctor, promoting justice, or supporting the agencies of the law—all these are in accord with accepted norms; helping the businessman make money is not. Even if the goal of business is formulated in broader terms—organizing the productive capacities of the country—many sociologists will doubt whether the contemporary American businessman is on the right track toward achieving it.

Indications of this attitude toward business are not difficult to find. Industrial sociologists usually focus their attention on the men and women in the trench lines of the production process; and, although this interest can be traced to traditional concern for the underdog, they nonetheless often find themselves being attacked as servants of exploitation (119).[1] Moreover, reviews of current work in the field of business frequently are defensive in tone (133). Concomitantly, most sociologists have tended to ignore many aspects of the business world. This has led to a paradoxical situation. A rough content analysis of the *Harvard Business Review* shows that the volume for 1928 contained one article dealing with the social sciences; interest in these fields steadily increased, however, so that, in the 1950s a typical volume devoted about one-third of its content to problems of social science. In contrast, an equally rough content analysis of the *American Journal*

[1] Numbers in parentheses refer to the Selected Bibliography at the end of this paper.

of Sociology reveals that up to 1950 there had been hardly any articles at all on business; more recently, however, at most one in ten articles has dealt with it.

The following pages review some of the ideas and data available for work on neglected aspects of the sociology of business.[2] The selection of materials is guided by two considerations. The main attention is on studies seldom included in sociological bibliographies; those in industrial sociology are ignored intentionally. Furthermore I concentrate on the idea of an "empirical analysis of action," a general orientation that will soon be more clearly delimited. I look at business as an intricate system of interlocking human activities. At one end, managers make decisions about production, pricing, and promotion; at the other end, consumers choose what to buy and what not to buy; and, along this line, individuals decide to join or to leave the organization and how much effort to put into their work. The consumer and the manager will be compared. (By "business," incidentally, I mean all the activities connected with the manufacture and distribution of goods, excluding farming and the free professions, but including banking and research development within industrial organizations.)

Emphasis on this orientation results in a temporary gap. A sociologist would regard business as a special object for organizational analysis. Yet the efforts in this direction come mainly from men in other fields. In their recent survey, March and Simon have developed a general outline in which the major sociological studies of organization find their place alongside studies of business organizations conducted by those in other disciplines (53). Conversely, Papandreou has systematically combed sociological publications to find out whether anything said there can broaden the economists' traditional "theory of the firm" (126). There still remains the need to look at business as a social system, both to see how far current social theory clarifies business practices and also to learn what new problems arise (to be attempted in a subsequent paper). At the moment it seems more fruit-

[2] I am indebted to Albert Gollin for bibliographical and editorial help in the preparation of this paper.

ful to start with the agents in management and in the market and to view organization as one determinant of their actions.

The Empirical Analysis of Action

The empirical study of individuals' choices or decisions, such as voting, buying, joining unions or other institutions, making investments, or committing suicide, has remained largely undeveloped. Even the matter of terminology is bothersome. The act of buying a particular brand of cigarettes is usually called a "choice." The action of a businessman who greatly expands the productive capacity of his firm is usually called a "decision." No one word refers to the long, drawn-out, and interlocking elements of the process by which a college student enrolls in a business school. We shall talk of action whenever we combine into one unit a goal-directed series of behavior that ends in a fairly distinguishable consummatory move. However, to avoid stuffiness, we shall often use words such as "choice" and "decision" interchangeably with "action."

There are three major ways of studying action. The first one focuses on the outcome: people can be divided into those who have and those who have not performed particular acts. Performance rates can then be studied for various groups, time periods, or situations. I shall call this the *distributive approach* (Durkheim's analysis of suicide rates is a classical example).

But it is also possible to concentrate directly on the actors: the agents, the performers. This leads to two further procedures. The one consists of describing the course of the act and making comparisons between the various ways in which the same end state is reached. This I shall call the *morphological approach*. The term is taken directly from Durkheim, who speaks of the morphology of suicide when he deals with the means by which people take their lives, the time it takes before they make the tragic move, etc.

The third type of analysis involves causal assessment. On the basis of available evidence we might, for instance, divide suicides according to whether they have been caused by failure in the personal sphere, or the occupational sphere, or both. In the case of crimes we might want to know whether seduction into crime by other people played a causal role. When a set of comparable acts is classified on the basis of some causal assessment made in each single case, I shall call it an *analytical approach*.

The difference between the morphological and analytical approaches can be shown in a study of the part played by friends and advertisements in the decisions of six hundred women to attend the movies (18). One set of findings dealt with the order in which these stimuli occurred and indicated that discussing the picture with friends usually preceded reading about it in magazines or newspapers (18, p. 193). We would call this a "morphological approach," because no causal assessment was made of which of those exposures was the more effective. In each case, however, the investigator and the subject assessed the relative influence of the advice of friends and the mass media (18, p. 179). Personal influence was found more effective in bringing about decisions either to attend or not to attend the movies. This, by definition, is an analytical approach.

The analytical approach raises a well-known controversy over the possibility of assessing the contribution of a specific element of an act to its final outcome. Those who deny this possibility usually insist that neither the investigators nor their respondents can really tell "why people act the way they do." This objection is a strange mixture of logical misunderstanding and empirical prejudice. The logical error lies in a faulty formulation of the problem. In a general form, the question "Why?" is, of course, unanswerable. Everything that has happened in the life of an individual can be considered a cause of his most recent act. But the competent student of, say, the buying act wants to know something else: he wants to know in what proportion of his cases a factor—an advertisement, the advice of a friend, or the shape of a cake of soap—has played a causal role. This focus on the causal impact of a specific element still leaves open a question of fact.

A man can, in principle, say whether he is going out because his wife has asked him to fetch something; but a girl who becomes engaged can hardly tell whether a similarity between her fiancé and her father has been crucial in her decision. Which factors can be causally assessed in this sense and which can not is an issue for empirical research; it will not be settled on logical grounds. Once this distinction is cleared up, there is at least the possibility that the empirical analysis of action will open up a vast area of descriptive facts that in the course of time may develop into more systematic knowledge.

In order to clarify the assessment procedure, I shall at first restrict myself to "external" elements, such as the role of advice, advertisements, etc. Pertinent studies proceed in four steps. First, one has to establish which cases are actually comparable. A smoker who has just changed his brand of cigarettes must be interviewed differently from one who has remained loyal to the same brand for the last ten years. Second, it is necessary to develop interviewing techniques that elicit enough information for the investigator to assess the role of the factor that interests him. For instance, experiments have shown that 2 per cent of the buyers answered the question "Why did you buy this brand?" with references to advertisements; when the question was changed more specifically to "What made you *start* using this brand?" 24 per cent spontaneously mentioned advertisements (1, p. 84). The third step is usually the most complicated. The investigator must make his assessment in each case: How reliable is it? Smith and Suchman have demonstrated that a number of different analysts agree quite well when they read the same cases and are asked to rate whether the role of a radio commercial was practically decisive, whether it had no importance, or whether it was somewhere in between (25). The fourth step provides the final result in terms of a statistical statement: *X* per cent of the cases were strongly influenced by a newspaper campaign, the advice of friends, or whatever the case may be.

A well-conducted study of this kind has interesting logical implications which cannot be considered here. A systematic discussion, with many examples, and drawing upon our joint experience, will be found in Zeisel's chapters on "Reason Analysis" (112). It is, however, important to see that the procedure coincides with a classical problem in the social sciences. In a famous discussion of the logic of the cultural sciences, Max Weber argued that it makes sense to ask how much weight one should assign to the causal role of a specific episode or person in the course of a larger historical sequence (111). With enough knowledge about all the surrounding circumstances and reasonable knowledge of comparable situations, one can perform a mental experiment and say that, with a certain probability, the sequence would have been different without the factor under investigation. In a footnote Weber adds that this procedure is applicable "not only in the domain of the usually so-called specialist discipline of history, but also in the 'historical' ascertainment of every individual event" (111, p. 166). A careful reading of his essay shows the complete parallel of his analysis with the first three steps outlined above. The fourth is a step particular to consumer research and similar statistical procedures. There the analyst may assume that, if he overrates the role of advertising in some cases, he will underrate it in others, so that the statistical result remains valid. Thus the statistical result is not so much affected by assessment errors as the individual case. Rossi, in his study of why families move, has given some inferential evidence on this point (109, chap. viii).

Both the morphological and the analytical approaches require that we think of actions as structures. In the essay mentioned above, Max Weber wrote about the necessity of assessing the "causal significance of individual components." The classification of these components (factors, elements) has since become a widespread concern. Frequently, graphs are used to locate them along a time line, indicating their interconnections by slings and arrows. One author might give a graph with eleven factors as an "incomplete scheme . . . for the purpose of orienting the reader" (99). Another might use thirteen graphs with more than a hundred elements to give "all the descriptive and theoretical constructs necessary for explaining and predicting the action of individual persons" (110). There is disagreement as to the grounds for these structural classifications. Parsons feels that "an act involves *logically* a number of aspects" (108). (Italics mine.) Other authors stress that such articulations depend upon the specific purpose of an investigation (105).

In reviewing the proposed list of relevant components of action, we find that one distinction is all-pervasive: between the elements of the environment and those residing in the actor. Following the old stimulus-disposition-response sequence, we shall call the latter "dispositions." The elements external to the actor we shall call "exposures," because the old word "stimulus" has acquired too narrow a connotation. An exposure in a more general sense can be the climate of opinion in a man's environment, the characteristic of a product he scans, channels of information he consults, etc. The variety of dispositions will be considered presently.

Let us, finally, combine the two main distinctions —the structure of an act and the way it can be analyzed. The components or elements may be external or internal to the actor, and they may either be singled out descriptively or be causally assessed. This gives the scheme shown in Figure 1.

	Described	*Causally Assessed*
External	Exposure	Influence
Internal	Disposition	Motive

FIGURE 1

The two specific terms in the first column have already been introduced. When a study has imputed a causal impact to an external *exposure,* I call this component an *influence.* When a study has imputed causal impact to a *disposition,* I will call it a *motive.* This is a restricted use of the word "motive" which is often applied to dispositions even though no causal assessment is involved, but failure to make some clear terminological distinction within the second line of our scheme has created a great deal of confusion in the literature.

The term "causally assessed" also is used in a restricted sense to be distinguished from other types of causal interpretation. A study found that "foreign travel experience counteracts self-interest, thus leading to a convergence of views among men with different self-interests" (36). The authors compared attitude rates among businessmen with different amounts of travel experience and carefully applied survey-analysis techniques to see whether foreign travel could really be considered a cause of this convergence. They *interpreted* a set of correlations. We could also interview businessmen who had changed their attitude—reciprocal trade was the issue—*assess* the role of foreign travel in each single case, and come up with a statistical figure as to the frequency of this influence. In the first case statistics *precedes* the interpretation; in the second case it *follows* the assessment (102).

We shall use studies of consumers to illustrate the general paradigm developed in this section. As examples of causal assessments I shall restrict myself for the time being to the consideration of exposures and influences. Before turning to disposition and motives, some further systematic discussion will be needed. Finally, managerial decisions will come under scrutiny.

Analysis of Buying as a Paradigm

DISTRIBUTIVE APPROACH

Every society keeps the records most relevant for its major values. It is not surprising, then, that in a market society purchase activities are among those for which we have the most abundant data. Some of these records are familiar even in the earliest tradition of social analysis, notably budgets divided into major consumption categories such as food, clothing, rent, and recreation. Buying rates of more specific commodities have escaped the attention of sociologists. Still they have possible utility for some of our standard topics; consider, for example, social stratification and the theory of reference groups.

The files of market-research organizations contain numerous studies showing that different social strata have different buying habits. Some of them reflect mere differences in available income. But others indicate variations in the whole experience patterns of different social strata. In a series of Austrian studies I was struck by finding that people of low income prefer sweet chocolate, fabrics with a rubbery touch, and strong-smelling flowers; upper-class consumers favored what one might call more demanding sensory experiences: bitter-dry tastes, irregular weaves, and less pungent fragrances. (The stereotype of the working man with the "loud" tie, and of the Ivy League student with the tweed jacket would fit in here.) One can give a more psychological explanation: the lower-class person is starved out for pleasant sense experiences; or a more sociological one: the upper-class individual exhibits his "sensual" wealth by conspicuous non-consumption of strong stimuli. The popular-music industry supplies continuous information on sales of records, performances on radio stations, and so on. Twenty years ago "hits" moved from the radio networks to records and jukeboxes (10). Today the claim is that they flow in the opposite direction, beginning with the local disk jockey and ending sometimes on a network. This affects the whole musical content of this all-pervasive commodity, because it makes a different social stratum the style-setters. While not strictly pertaining to purchases, some market studies show significant differences in standards of judgments. Radio and television commercials despised by the educated strata are considered interesting and desirable by those on the lower end of the socioeconomic scale (20, p. 83). And from a study of dieting we know that, among women of the same actual weight, the tendency to consider themselves overweight shows a high positive correlation with socioeconomic status (23, p. 340).

The importance of reference groups in buying behavior has recently been reviewed by a symposium of marketing students (6). I call special attention to a study which permits weighing the importance of the primary environment against varying kinds of personal attitudes: the popularity of a beverage among one's friends can override his desire to stay slim and his moral objections to the beverage; but, if he dislikes its taste, he is not likely to drink it even if his friends do (6, p. 223). An inferential use of saving rates belongs here. Duesenberry (9) tried to improve classical economic theory on the relation between saving and income by developing the idea that the tendency to save depends upon one's income relative to his primary environment rather than upon absolute income. The more people one knows who have a standard of living higher than one's own, the more likely one is to spend all earnings immediately rather than to save. Part of the statistical evidence is a survey which shows, perhaps contrary to the expectations of some, that within each income level Negroes save more than whites (9, p. 50). Duesenberry explains this in terms of the relative isolation of the Negro community: contact with the top income groups is more frequent among the whites.

Buying habits can also be used to characterize social position and conceptions of role. Stone has shown that isolated city dwellers prefer to buy in small stores because this provides them with personal contacts (27). A number of activities are considered the sign of a good housewife by some women and old-fashioned by others: home sewing (23, p. 313), doing one's own laundry (1, p. 275), and shunning instant coffee (14). One interested in the drift away from the traditional family will find here quantitative data which should permit rather precise differentiations. To say the least, it would be worthwhile to encourage a number of master's theses in which this kind of material is sifted for sociological implications.

Morphological Approach

A good illustration comes from a study by Katona and Mueller (17). They carried out detailed interviews with buyers of durable goods (e.g., refrigerators, television sets, etc.) in order to see how deliberate were their purchases. They developed several dimensions of deliberation: a) the extent of circumspectness, indicated by the length of the planning period and the number of alternative purchases considered; b) the extent of information-seeking activity, indicated by the number of stores visited, advertisements read, the advice looked for; and c) the number of features—style, operating costs, service arrangements, etc.—considered. Out of these and a number of other aspects they constructed an over-all index of deliberation.[3]

[3] They discovered the greatest amount of deliberation in the middle strata. People of low education did not have the critical ability or initiative to avail themselves of all sources of information, although their low income would have made a careful choice urgent. At the other extreme, buyers on the highest socioeconomic level were less deliberate than the middle groups, presumably because a specific expenditure assumed less importance for them. The deliberateness of the middle class fits well with other known characteristics of it.

A somewhat similar morphological feature is the pattern of hesitation in a purchase. In a Roper study, automobile buyers were asked on repeated occasions how soon they were likely to buy their next car. The respondents were crudely classified according to whether they planned to buy "right now," within the next six months, or still later. People oscillated greatly on their "nearness to purchase" from one interview to the next, the interviews being at intervals of three months. While obviously many moved forward, a large number had less immediate plans the second time than at the first. The number of such "two steps forward, one back" sequences will depend partly upon the size of the expenditure. But it seems partly related to how easily the wisdom of a purchase can be decided upon even after it has been made. This is a distinction which hints at a larger general classification of action. Every smoker knows very soon after he has lighted it whether he has bought a good cigar, but it takes a longer time to assess the merits of a new pipe; and whether we have chosen the right occupation may take us years to find out.

This leads to the general idea that expected experiences with a purchase should be considered a part of its structure. The anticipation that the choice will be difficult to check might make for greater concern with other people's opinions. Inversely, the anticipation of other people's reactions might affect the length or character of deliberation.[4] Some inferential evidence on this point comes from a series of experiments by Bauer (2). He showed that what the subjects remembered of a speech on teachers' salaries was affected by the kind of audience to which they were supposed to report subsequent to their own exposure: when told they would summarize the speech for a group of teachers, they remembered more of the arguments in favor of raising salaries; when told they would report to a citizen's group dedicated to economies, they remembered more of the arguments against raising salaries.

The Analytical Approach

We often lament how difficult it is to predict human behavior. But it is almost as hard to evaluate the effect of past behavior. Amid all

---

[4] This point was suggested to me by my colleague, Amitai Etzioni.

today's turmoil of propaganda and advertising we can rarely tell whether a specific "campaign" has reached its goal. One of the devices which has been tried is to interview people who have performed a desired act. Can we trace in their retrospection the influence we are interested in? I am the co-author of a recent study which assessed the comparative role of personal advice and of advertising (18). Our conclusion was that the former is stronger. Assuming that we were right, then our statistical results could be developed in many directions. In what situations and with what kinds of people is personal influence especially strong or weak? Who are influential? (We had something to say about this in chap. xv.) Kadushin (98) investigated how clients of a psychological consulting service came to use it. He found that working-class people were the most dependent on others even to become aware that they had difficulties. Caplow and Raymond showed the importance of the commercial detail man in inducing the doctor to use a new pharmaceutical product (7). But at the same time a group of Columbia sociologists were able to show that this influence is greater among isolated doctors than among those who have frequent contact with colleagues even within the same cities (8).

There is something tantalizing about all these studies. On the one hand, one feels that man in the modern world is the object of continuous "natural" experiments. Why pass up such a rich source of potential knowledge? On the other hand, we can not be sure that even the best interview technique can successfully assess the causal role of all the "stimuli" we are subject to. (Rossi has provided some encouraging verification in the case of residential mobility [109].) To put the dilemma in still a different form, people are similar to mice in that they run through mazes all day long having to decide whether to move right or left; but they are different from mice inasmuch as they are aware of their cues and can report on what happened to them. But how different are mice and men from the point of view of the social scientist who looks for reliable data? Consumer studies, carefully watched and guided, might help us to answer this question.

Our last simile was meant to serve a methodological purpose. But, taken even facetiously, it does raise a serious substantive question. To what extent are such studies socially dangerous either because they are used for exploitative purposes or because they overlook those aspects of human behavior which are not accessible to manipulation? Some sociologists have given serious attention to the "weakness of the consumer," and reference to their publications is very much in place here (11, 21). I have concentrated so far on influences; it is time now to turn to motives in the sense of our aforementioned scheme.

A Digression on Disposition Concepts

Before going further, the role of dispositions in empirical action analysis has to be clarified. I have already referred to the distinction between motive as a causally assessed disposition and the merely descriptive use of terms like "needs" or "goals," which are often summarized under the catchall heading of "motivation." No general classification of disposition concepts exists. An author is usually interested in one of them; he tries to define it carefully and then gives a list of comparisons

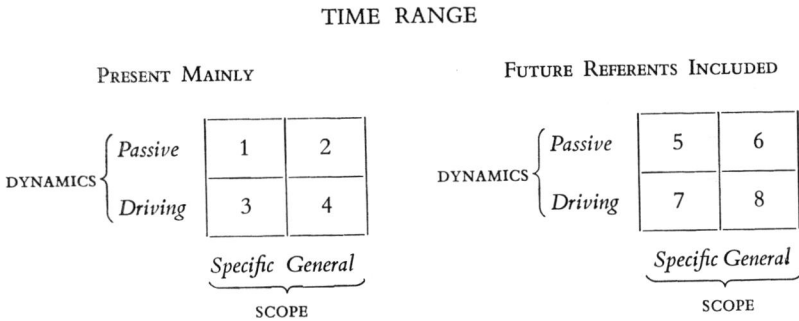

TIME RANGE

FIGURE 2

with "related concepts." Thus Allport concentrates on attitudes and discusses how they differ from values, interests, opinions, etc. (97). Kluckhohn focuses on values and tries to differentiate them from attitudes, needs, goals, beliefs, etc. (100). The literature along this line is practically endless.

But, by starting from shifting linguistic usages, one misses just those distinctions which lead to essential variations in research procedures and in interpretations. It is more fruitful to bring out the dimensions along which distinctions have been proposed so that the intent of various authors becomes more comparable and the terminology loses its importance. A scrutiny of various texts shows that three dimensions dominate the discussion. One is generality and specificity (e.g., a personality trait that can be exhibited in many substantive spheres versus an interest usually directed toward a limited object). Another may be described as degree of directiveness (e.g., an attitude toward versus a desire for something, the former being more of the passive, the second more of the driving kind). A third dimension relates to the time perspective (e.g., a plan or an expectation spans the future; an urge or a perceptual bias focuses on the present). If we dichotomize these three dimensions of substantive scope, dynamics, and time range, we get eight combinations which can serve classificatory purposes and at the same time show what other aspects are involved in the linguistic tradition of these disposition concepts (Fig. 2). (In a more detailed discussion the three dimensions would be treated as continuous, so that finer distinctions could be made.)

Most terms have been used differently by various authors, and most readers will attach their own private associations to them. This should be remembered in reading a few examples that illustrate the relatively simple three-dimensional scheme, which for our purpose seems useful.

1 *Preferences* as for specific foods and *opinions* on specific issues are specific, passive, and current.
2 *Traits* like broad-mindedness, more general *attitudes* like economic liberalism, as well as such "frames of reference" as looking at issues from a "businessman's point of view" are general, passive, and current.
3 What are usually called *wants* or needs, like being hungry or looking for a new car to replace a worn-out one, are specific, driving, and current.
4 More *directional traits* like vitality and energy or aggressiveness may be described as general, driving, and current.
5 *Expectations* as to future prices and customer demands that are important in modern economic analysis are typical examples of the specific, passive, future-oriented dispositions.
6 *Tendencies* to consider longer chains of possible consequences and *inclinations*

like optimism come to mind as examples of the more general, passive, and future-oriented dispositions.

7 Investment *intentions,* occupational *plans,* and schemes for getting promoted to an impending executive vacancy may be described as specific, driving, and future-oriented.

8 The ubiquitous term "motivation" should become less ambiguous here. In the present paper I shall restrict the term "motivation" to a disposition of rather *general scope* and with the implication that it *directs* its bearer toward activities that bridge the present and the *future.*

Type 8 is the one most relevant for present purposes, but, as a by-product, a number of worthwhile distinctions can be distinguished. Types 2, 4, and 6 are usually lumped together as traits. We can assume that businessmen are more politically conservative (Type 2) than, say, university professors and more energetic (Type 4). Whether the businessmen are more optimistic about future events (Type 6) than professors is hard to guess and might change according to circumstances. The specific (odd numbered) dispositions are more pertinent in the present context. Types 5 and 7, expectations and plans, have acquired importance in recent econometric studies of business intentions (54). They can both be introduced as variables in time-series studies. There the double role of time becomes especially clear; for any expectation we have to know at what time it is held and to what future period it refers. The relation between the "passive" expectation and the "driving" plan is complex. While plans lead to action, expectations affect plans; we know from voting studies that intentions often color expectations (3). Type 3, wants or needs, are traditional in consumer studies. Types 5 and 7 often seem more accessible to simple interviews than Type 3; the latter were the entering wedge for projective techniques. Type 1 includes the typical objects of polls.

Thus we see that even this simple classification of dispositions leads to differences in problems and research techniques which can be derived from the position of the types in the dimensional scheme. Additional variations can be handled more casually because they do not seem to be of much consequence for our subject matter; this holds for the means-end relation, for instance, and the separation of a state (angry) from a trait (irascible). The distinction between physiological and culturally induced wants will become relevant at one point only. But one other complication has to be introduced. It came about when anthropologists and sociologists began to scan these concepts of disposition. A goal may be pursued or a selection made with or without the feeling that doing so is morally desirable or will be socially rewarded. This leads to the notion of norm or value. All the categories listed above can take on a normative element, although some may do so more easily than others. Intentions (Type 7) and wants (Type 3) seem to be more often "affected by public interest" than expectations (Type 5) and frames of reference (Type 2). For most purposes it is enough to refer to the normative element when needed, without doubling the terminology.

Every one of the eight types of dispositions can become a motive in the study of specific acts. One finds in the literature statements to the effect that people are motivated by optimism, by a specific goal, by a cultural orientation, by an expectation, etc. Inasmuch as these refer to concrete acts where the causal role of any of the dispositions is assessed, the phrasing is consistent with our terminology. The term "motivation," on the other hand, will be reserved for a rather broad, driving, and future-oriented disposition of Type 8 in our scheme. Often it is used in a much broader and looser sense, sometimes being applied to all dispositions, sometimes to all those of great scope or all those with strong directive implications. In references to such usage in this paper the word "motivation" will be put in quotation marks, but, with or without quotation marks, the term will refer to a described disposition which at best has a good probability of becoming a motive in a specific act.

Consumer "Motivation"

THE THREE APPROACHES REVISITED

Introducing dispositions as empirical variables has two consequences for the distributive approach: either these dispositions can appear as correlates of consumer behavior or they can be studied in their own right. In the heyday of radio daytime serials there were many opportunities to study whether listeners and non-listeners differed in something more than the familiar demographic characteristics of education and age; the findings were largely negative (15). Commercial research organizations have sometimes claimed that they were able to use existing personality tests successfully; the ubiquitous *F*-scale is said to correlate with the desire for a powerful car, the compulsiveness of housewives with the number of cleansers they use, and so on. Occasionally, one finds a new notion, such as "readiness to spend money" or "susceptibility to advertising."

No recorded study traces the effects of past satisfactions, but it is not difficult to imagine the form such a study might take. If, for instance, people kept records of their attendance at the movies, it might be possible to see whether the average elapsed time between visits is affected by satisfaction with the last experience. The role of expectations in saving has been extensively studied by Katona; his main interest is how saving relates to actual changes in income. In one study, for instance, he shows that, contrary to economic theory, an increase in income may result in a reduction of savings; this is likely to happen when people consider the increase a signal of future advancement and make sudden shifts in their whole style of life (16).

What if the dispositions themselves become the dependent variables to be investigated? Strangely enough, I have not been able to find an existing empirical study along these lines. To my knowledge, the distribution of such motivations as Veblen's conspicuous consumption has never been measured in different social groups. Lewin's level of aspiration seems also to have been ignored in consumer studies. Inversely, the issue recently raised in Galbraith's "affluent society" belongs here (118). His argument is that an expanding economy which at the same time resists governmental planning depends too much upon the creation of new consumer wants; this diverts too large a part of the national income toward private consumption and away from social services. Assuming that the argument is correct, what could research do about it? How much awareness is there of the issue Galbraith raises? How do Americans want to cope with it?[5] If there is little knowledge, could the public be informed through educational programs? Is it possible to shift the desire for personal possessions toward a greater concern with social improvements? Incidentally, some comparative studies would be highly desirable. In England and Scandinavia we seem to find a different balance among economic expansion, the desire for gadgets, and the neglect of social services.

When it comes to assessing dispositions as determinants of specific purchases, new problems arise. Ostensibly, products serve specific ends, and it seems quite meaningless to ask people for what purpose they bought a refrigerator or a can of food. But, because there are so many styles and brands of the same product, one can not discount the possibility that there are collateral needs to be satisfied. Voting studies can best explain the issues involved. If someone shifts his intention to vote from one candidate to another, two different processes may be involved. The voter may retain his standard of judgment—for instance, that preservation of peace is most important—but he may have acquired information which leads him to believe that another candidate is more likely to serve this end. Or the voter may have preserved his opinion of the candidates but have developed the opinion that, let us say, domestic economic issues are really more important than international affairs. A shift in brand preferences on the part of an automobile buyer can be analyzed in the same way: his attitudes toward speed may remain the same, but his opinion as to which car is faster could change; or his opinions of different makes may remain the same, while, for some reason, he comes to attach more importance to roominess than to speed.

Once dispositions are introduced as empirical variables, we can con-

---

[5] I prevailed upon a polling agency in 1957 to ask a national sample whether they approved or disapproved of continuous changes in car design. One-half disapproved. But, asked how these changes should be curtailed, only 10 per cent thought that consumers themselves could exercise the necessary discipline; 60 per cent wanted self-regulation on the part of the industry; and 30 per cent favored governmental intervention. Besides the astonishing lack of confidence people had in themselves and in one another, the most noticeable finding was a social difference: the lower-income groups were relatively much more in favor of governmental regulation.

sider explicitly the mutual relations between exposure and dispositions, the "inner" and the "outer" components of the various schemata mentioned above. A hungry person sees more food elements in an ink-blot test; a picture of a luscious cake can evoke appetite. The only way to disentangle these two processes is to follow them through time.[6] This is done in a so-called panel study, the general outlines of which I assume are known (106). Typically, such studies result in the following kind of finding: people who are interested in politics at one time are found to talk about it more in a subsequent interview; but amount of talk at Time I is also predictive of greater interest at Time II. It is possible to weigh the relative importance of the two elements in a sample of observations.

The applicability of these procedures to the act of buying has been stressed by Roshwalb (24). The best examples come from studies in which people are repeatedly asked whether they use a product and whether they are exposed to its advertising. In sample surveys answers to these two items are always highly correlated. Through panel studies one can show that considerable numbers of people begin to pay attention to the advertisement for a particular brand only *after* they have bought the product; the presumable explanation is that they look for reassurance or want to compare their experiences with those of others. The evocative effect of advertising on buying and the directive effect of owner interest on exposure appear in very different combinations for various products and advertising programs. The material available in the files of some commercial organizations deserves to be further analyzed from a theoretical point of view.[7]

[6] Kurt Lewin assigned "valences" to the environment and "tensions" to the actor but got into great logical difficulties because he did not place them in a time sequence (103). Bilkey, one of his followers, has measured people's desire for certain products and their resistance to spending money; their actual purchases turned out to be a kind of resultant of these two indexes (4, 5). Bilkey speaks of the effect of a negative and a positive "valence." However, he overlooks the fact that he does not really touch on the critical issue — the interrelation of a "valence" and a "tension." It is also doubtful whether the simple attitudes measured in this study really correspond to Lewin's concepts.

[7] This whole idea has been applied to a more traditional sociological topic, the mutual effects of friendship and similarity of beliefs (104).

Motivation Research (MR)

Suppose now that the following question is raised in a somewhat vague way: What kind of dispositions can act as motives to buy a product and what features of the product (or its advertisement) are likely to activate these dispositions? In other words, instead of studying the interrelations between dispositions and exposure over time, the potential interplay of motives and influences (the "effective features" of the product and its advertising) is made the central concern. This idea led to a development called "motivation research" (MR) which became quite a fad in commercial circles. It deserves a moment's attention because it is not easy to evaluate properly and because it has recently found a parallel in the work of social scientists studying the "motivation" of businessmen. Gardner describes the MR program succinctly:

> "Such explorations must take into account the character of the product (the human needs it serves and the particular way it does so), the dimensions employed in evaluating brands of such a product, and where the particular brand stands on these dimensions" (12).

Traditional projective devices—ranging from sentence completions to the interpretation of unstructured pictures or the narrative elaboration of partially told stories—are the standard tools of MR. All the material, however, is so selected that the elicited associations are as closely related to the product as possible. The material is often interpreted in terms of whatever "depth psychology" the analyst is acquainted with. Thus certain situations, like flying or fighting for an insurance claim, create anxiety, and so the stewardess and the insurance salesman become regressive mother and father substitutes. In other cases the "product-consumer relation" is described in more modest terms, the emphasis being on connections that are likely to be overlooked. Thus home sewing can be drudgery or artistic self-expression; the suit salesman should be serious because we need his assurance of quality we can not really judge; the shoe salesman should be friendly because we feel embarrassed about our stockinged feet.[8]

In principle there is nothing wrong with such studies of product-related dispositions; but in the turmoil of commercial research the controversy over MR has led to two rather dangerous claims. Because projective tests and the detailed interviews that often accompany them are expensive, small samples have been used; and they have been defended on the grounds that they are sufficient for such refined material. This might be so if the problem were only whether, for some people somewhere, certain complex dispositions are organized around specific products. But information about frequency and distribution, necessary for practical purposes, requires, of course, the same sampling standards that are used in other types of field research. (The issue should not be confused with the controversy over clinical versus statistical methods in the diagnosis of *individual* cases.) This leads to the interesting question of whether some projective techniques can be adapted to mass surveys. I think so, but the procedure must be adapted to the specific problem on hand. Whether a particular brand of a product has low prestige can be found out by asking which brand the respondent would serve a guest; whether a product is related to childhood experiences might be approached by asking of whom the characters in an advertisement are reminiscent; often a sentence-completion test can be made simple enough for doorstep use (19).

Even more dangerous than the sampling problem is the confusion between the existence of certain dispositions and the question as to whether they are really motives—whether they play a causal role in purchases. In the commercial literature there is no evidence that people have even tried to assess the causal role of such action components, let alone to demonstrate the success of policies based on MR. As a matter of fact, in most cases the evidence for the mere existence of alleged dispositions is dubious. Even such a careful reviewer as Newman says

---

[8] To my knowledge there is only one book which gives a picture of what the MR practitioner really does. Newman presents six very detailed examples, with interviews with the client and the research people (23).

of an MR study that "the interviews indicated that the American housewife represents a good potential for increased coffee consumption" (23, p. 171). It is almost inconceivable that the actual data could support such a claim.[9]

One curious outcome of this MR game deserves special mention. In spite of the small samples, enough studies have accumulated by now to show convincingly that people form quite unexpected stereotypes about products: certain makes of cars are considered young or female; certain brands of cigarettes are held to be appropriate for people in particular occupations. In part these stereotypes may be due to actual observation and in part to the advertising policy of the manufacturers. But some of the "brand images" (12) are rather surprising; for instance, that particular brands of liquor are considered more appropriate for one or another type of personality. In the bewildering mass of available goods and brands, the consumer can not remember all their features, let alone judge them; as a result, he forms vague images to orient his buying decisions.

In the commercial literature these observations are only reported, usually with the implication that the advertiser should take them into account. The really interesting question, however, is the origin of such images, and on this problem hardly any serious research has been done. A few leads are available. Wiggins has shown that consumers have a tendency to project their own characteristics onto the products they own; consequently, for instance, men and women differ much more in their imagery of their own cars than of other makes. It also seems

[9] One of the few exceptions is Haire's much-quoted study that housewives consider a woman who uses instant coffee as sloppy (14). A few other efforts to provide evidence for the existence of dispositions can be gleaned from a bibliographical review by Horsley Smith (26). Sociologists who are interested in this problem of evidence for complex mass attitudes but who dislike working with commercial data might try their skill on two texts: Sayles and Strauss's description of the way in which workers feel torn between loyalty to the union and gratitude to the employer for giving them a job (129) and Gardner's description of ambivalence toward big corporations — they are admired for their power and efficiency but need checking by government and labor, which in turn are distrusted (13).

that some differences, such as sex, are more closely related to these stereotypes than are others, such as age. Sometimes it is possible to compare the image of the ideal product with the images of a number of specific brands; it is claimed that, the larger the discrepancy between the ideal and the concrete stereotypes, the lower the sales of the brand. The problem of imagery is not new, of course; racial and occupational stereotypes have been studied before. But having this extensive material on commercial products might help clarify many of the unsolved problems in this field.

Surprisingly enough, we shall encounter the MR idea once more, although not under this name, when we now review the empirical analysis of action of managers.

Managerial and Consumer Action Compared

How much does an outsider really know about what businessmen do? Throughout the preparation of this report I have found myself troubled by the lack of such firsthand knowledge. Having scanned a great deal of descriptive literature, I want to single out two books which were helpful. Gordon describes the "business corporation as organized human activity shaped to the achieving of certain basic common purposes through procedures that are chosen, devised, guided and progressively modified by the personalities, major and minor, who are themselves the cogs and levers on the machine" (71). This sentence characterizes the institutional view of the author—a view which greatly helps the reader to become acquainted with the inter-relations among the different parts of a major business organization. To complement this "systemic" approach, we have Copeland's description of the executive at work (32). For many years Copeland was the research director of the Harvard Business School, and in his book he summarizes his observations on the kind of decisions the businessman is called upon to make and what he should watch out for when he makes them. While his descriptions do not have the intellectual import of Chester Barnard's classic (64), they give a more vivid

picture of an executive's daily life.[10] The more specific studies reviewed in the following sections and the reflections derived from them
will show that this descriptive literature is beginning to give way to
conceptualizations and statements of problems sufficiently sharp to
suggest systematic research.

Contrary to the treatment of consumer data, this discussion of
businessmen's decisions does not have a section on the distributive
approach. Such an effort, in fact, would be tantamount to giving a
sociological foundation to contemporary economics. Findings on
variations of investments with the business cycle, on the empirical
relations between price and demand, on the fluctuations of research
expenses with changing tax legislation, and endless other aggregate
data of this kind would have to be interpreted in the light of present
sociological knowledge; or they might be added to the fund of data
which a future Summa Sociologica will have to take into account.
Interdisciplinary enterprises of this kind are increasing in number and
scope; a good example can be found in a symposium on the non-
economic elements in Keynesian theory, where the contributions of
Lekachman (123) and Vickrey (132) are especially pertinent. But a
review of this trend would require a paper of its own.

I shall therefore confine myself to the direct approach to managerial
decisions: their morphological structure and their causal determinants.
One general remark will make it unnecessary to repeat the same
observation at several points. I often state or imply the need for statisti-

---

[10] Occasionally, efforts have been made to develop more precise instruments to
describe managerial activities. None of them has led very far. Stogdill and Shartle
tested the reliability and validity of a work-analysis form. They use it at one point to
compare navy officers and businessmen by the time spent in contact with other persons, in individual efforts, and in major responsibilities (60, p. 45). Carlson has ex-
perimented with techniques to record "executive behavior" along somewhat the same
lines (31). He attempts some generalization by showing on what topics executives
call in larger groups and when they confer with subordinates alone. His interest
centers, however, on the use of his technique as a diagnostic device to help the boss
increase his efficiency, and therefore his material is not very pertinent here. Still his
sixth chapter on "communication analysis" is a good starting point for further efforts.

cal information beyond the study of individual cases. In the analytical approach this is easily justified; we want to know how frequent certain influences and motives are. A morphological observation is often interesting in itself, especially if it has not been made before. But, in the long run, a generalization requires one of two possible extensions. We want to know either whether one kind of pattern is more successful than another in reaching the goal toward which an action is undertaken or whether it is useful to learn which kind of people tend to make what kind of moves. In regard to consumer studies this will be easily conceded. When it comes to managerial decisions, their unique character is often emphasized. But modern economic developments increasingly create situations where "managers" become a set comparble to "consumers." Large corporations have hundreds of managers with considerable independence; as a result, the central agency must analyze and evaluate their activities in the generalized form in which businessmen have long considered their consumers. The growth of nationalized industries in western Europe will most likely lead to a similar need for knowing the probable outcomes of various patterns of decision occurring under varying conditions of institution and personnel. It is true that at present few such data are available. But this makes it all the more necessary to keep the statistical implications in mind, even when individual cases are under scrutiny.

The Morphology of Managerial Decisions

A good starting point is found in recent efforts to loosen up the traditional notion of "rational choice," of which Herbert Simon's writings provide a characteristic illustration (59).[11] In classical economic theory the elements of rational choice are: the economic agent (the firm or the consumer) faces a set of alternatives, knows the consequences of

[11] I recommend especially the introduction to the various sections of his collection of essays, *Models of Man,* which can be understood by a reader even if he knows no mathematics. Simon's basic ideas recur and are elaborated in all his writings listed in the appended Bibliography.

each, and can rank the utility all the possible outcomes have for him. The choice consists in maximizing this utility. Simon points out that this scheme must be made more realistic in two respects. First, the actor does not really know all the alternatives; he must find them out, and, for this purpose, a period of search is necessary. Second, the actor does not know all the consequences, and he has neither the time nor the skill to figure them out. As a result of both these difficulties, he can not really maximize his utility. He stops his search and makes a decision when he has found an alternative which is "viable," even if, from the point of view of an all-knowing observer, it is by no means optimal.

This is an ingenious analysis, permitting a mathematical formulation related to and enlarging traditional mathematical economics. But, seen from another side, it is an application to more complex business decisions of morphological categories which are traditional in the empirical analysis of the consumer's choices. In 1956 Simon and his associates published one of the first detailed statements: "Observation of a Business Decision" (34). Apologetically they wrote in their conclusion that they did not "wish to try to transform one swallow into a summer by generalizing too far from a single example of a decision process." But why, it might be asked, did they not take notice of the thousand and one swallows nesting in similar publications by students of consumers? The notion of a search is very much akin to the shopping of the housewife or the deliberation and hesitation of the car-buyer.

This similarity points to an entirely new area of investigation. At what point, for instance, is the search stopped? When time pressure makes a move unavoidable or when further search becomes too expensive? Is its duration affected more by the personality and experience of the deciding executives or by structural arrangements such as the composition of committees and the number of internal interest groups involved in the decision? How is the search initiated? Because some episode brings an issue to the fore (e.g., an accident in the case of safety equipment) or because of the anticipatory thinking of a responsible agent? In the light of informed hindsight, how many consequences of the decisions were considered and how many overlooked?"[12]

The time span over which a decision is to become operative lends itself to worthwhile observations. Gort has pointed out that estimates about future conditions will be made more superficially the later they are likely to come into play (41). This has an interesting parallel to a well-known source of trouble in all private planning: to endow the future with the concreteness of the present. Dahl and Lindblom have dwelt on the notion of incrementalism (35, p. 82); applied to the analysis of decision, it leads to a classification in terms of whether a course of action is mapped out over a considerable stretch of a future road or whether one proceeds largely by trial and error, making adjustments as things develop.

As with consumer's choices, the links between an earlier managerial decision and subsequent ones are functionally related. This becomes highlighted when comparable moves are isolated and concentrated through some institutional arrangement. In Norway, after the last war, different government agencies decided on the allocation of raw materials, level of wages, and many other components of the process of production. Barton had occasion to interview the members of the "industry-directorate" which gave or refused import licenses and learned that at the beginning of their activities they were greatly worried by the lack of economic criteria (29). After a while, however, they made their allocation with increasing self-assurance. But what they had learned from previous experiences were not the economic consequences of decisions but ways, rather, of avoiding trouble with various power groups and ways of living with the hostilities the allocations invariably elicited. In other words, only empirical studies can show what and how much a businessman can "learn from experience."

---

[12] In an unpublished observation a major American corporation is reported to have given names to its system of salary grading, which facilitated promotional policy within the company, transfers from one division to another, etc. But, at the same time, the new system created considerable difficulties in communities dominated by the factories of this company. There social life was affected by people's tendency to classify each other according to the internal grading system of the company which was both more visible than income per se and a more permissible topic of discussion.

In a sequence of appointments, for instance, the top man may become increasingly aware of what a job requires without developing better criteria for selecting the right man. Inversely, an executive may not be able to change certain shortcomings in his personality, but perhaps he can learn to invent administrative arrangements which reduce the difficulties he would otherwise create.

Decisions of businessmen have a broad range of targets: pricing goods, employing people, opening up new resources. We can speculate for a moment on the difference between, say, pricing and investment decisions. Because the latter are more momentous, they might be reserved for men higher in the hierarchy; because the former require guesses about consumer reactions, they might bring men to the fore with a reputation for good hunches. A bad decision on pricing can be remedied by a changed advertising policy, whereas a bad one on investment is probably more often irreversible. What consequences does this have for the status, the security, and the personal relations of the officers involved or for the institutional devices to allocate blame?[13]

This leads, finally, to an interesting border area between the empirical study of action and organizational analysis. I found two examples in the literature in which administrative phenomena were explicitly derived from laws of individual behavior. March and Simon surmised a "Gresham's law" of planning (53, p. 185): when a person has a choice between routine tasks and duties requiring inventiveness, he will tend to give precedence to the routine. From this they concluded that, if inventiveness is to be built into an organization, it is necessary to set up special departments for development, the members of which are prohibited from performing routine tasks and in which only planning activities are rewarded. Gouldner assumed a law which

---

[13] When long-playing records became feasible, two systems were developed: a smaller disk with 45 rpm promoted by the Radio Corporation of America and a larger one, with 33½ rpm promoted by the Columbia Broadcasting System. Much could be said for both kinds, but the c.b.s. type finally won out. On what grounds did the experts in the two companies make their differing bets? What were the internal consequences of the outcome? Is it known, even in retrospect, why one system proved more successful? The determinants as well as the consequences of a decision could be studied in this case.

might be called the decreasing marginal utility of conformity: "Repeated identical acts of conformity increase or reinforce the expectation of conformity; later conforming actions are worth less than earlier ones in terms of the rewards they elicit." Gouldner gives examples from various areas of human experience which make this law plausible. On the organizational level he derives from it "a vicious cycle of bureaucratization. That is, the more formal rules there are governing action, the more conforming actions will be devalued in that they will yield smaller increments of appreciation or gratitude which can motivate reciprocity, and the more the rules will be further elaborated and enforced to prevent the decline in motivation from impairing the organization" (42, 424–26).

Determinants of Managerial Decisions

A few studies have provided statistical information on the economic intentions entering into major business decisions. Katona and Morgan report, for example, that, in locating a plant, businessmen are guided more by considerations of proximity to markets than by the proximity to raw materials (48). Decisions to invest in plant expansion less often occur as a result of expected increase in consumer demand than as a result of a steady policy of expansion and a desire to maintain or improve the present standing of the firm relative to competitors. Modigliani and Balderston obtained reports from business firms on three points: the investments they intended to make, the investments they actually made, and the explanations of discrepancies when these occurred (54). They found that a change in the outlook for sales was the single most important reason given for not carrying out intentions. Fortunately, the same study also contained information on sales expectations actually held by these firms at the time of the two interviews. Thus it was possible statistically to correlate trends in investment plans and in sales figures. The aggregate correlations and the reasons given by the businessmen in retrospective interviews supported each other.

More intricate problems are brought up by Machlup in a discussion of marginal analysis and empirical research (51). According to economic theory, a businessman should so establish his production that the cost of producing one further unit will just balance the revenue to be expected from its sale. Machlup criticizes a number of studies made by interview which purport to show that businessmen are actually guided more by their past experience than by their future expectations. His counter-argument is that the questionnaires were inadequate and that the investigators were confused by the terminology of the businessmen, which is at variance with economic theory, whereas their practice is not. Machlup does not make any concrete suggestions for research, but his paper gives a good picture of the task involved if one wants to test a complex theory with empirical data. (I might mention, in passing, a study of how taxes affect business decisions which provides vivid raw material but lacks analytic skill [39].)

Paralleling the preceding discussion of consumer's choices, there is the question of what would correspond to personal influence. Concerning managerial decisions, where there is greater variety and complexity, it is not immediately clear what these influences might be. I suggest three possible influences: informal groups, the relation of statuses, and visibility. As Kornhauser has pointed out, the reluctance of business managers to submit themselves to study by outsiders has compounded the tendency of social scientists to carry out studies where material is easily accessible (121). As a result, we continue to investigate informal groups of workers in the factory but know hardly anything about how these groups function in management. Yet relevant questions can be easily raised. In making their decisions, to what extent do executives rely on consultation within their company and to what extent are they influenced by their friends outside the company?[14] What is the role of professional consultants? There is undoubtedly something resembling a "kitchen cabinet" on the top level of many companies; what is the relation of it as a source of influence to the official hierarchy? In which situations does this in-

---

[14] In a Harvard symposium the owner of a small company described how he systematically seeks out the advice of his business friends all over the country. None of the participating "big shots" touched on this point (38).

fluence come into play? Has any major businessman produced a document comparable to Rosenman's account of *Working with Roosevelt* (58)? Some of the autobiographies of businessmen could be scrutinized for indications of such influences by small groups and persons (33). A great deal of work lies ahead if the final goal is systematic knowledge. An inkling of the complexity of the materials is provided, for example, by a series of reports which Guetzkow has made on his analysis of tape-recorded decision-making conferences (44, 45). He focused on the conditions under which the participants terminate their deliberations in consensus or in disagreement. He eventually used up to a hundred measures in order to describe the type of problems at issue, the way the participants behaved, their personal relations, and the final decisions—findings which are too complex to be reported here but which deserve careful attention.

The business literature occasionally contains very suggestive passages, such as Oxenfeldt's discussion of the type of influences to which an executive might be subjected when he makes a decision about pricing (55). Different points of view emerge from the production and the sales departments, and, in reaching a compromise, the top executive must take into account the social relations between his top men (in addition, of course, to making a final economic judgment). Such vivid and systematic descriptions could well be a starting point for useful empirical studies. Oxenfeldt's formulation that "prices do not simply happen; people set them" (55, p. 109) is a good motto for a sociological approach to all kinds of financial decisions. His materials also show that position and status within the firm have a part in affecting the final decision. Some of those, such as the staff-line problem, belong to the traditional repertoire of the industrial sociologist (42, and the literature quoted there). Others, such as the study of technical research people and personnel experts in business organization, are of more recent vintage (57). There has been little systematic study of the social research departments which are now being organized in large corporations. Mann has reported an interesting experiment which shows that research findings on employee morale are successfully used only if they are discussed in detail with the business managers (52). Other aspects of research as one of the determinants of decisions have yet to be looked at. For example, allocations for advertising are made repeatedly and under comparable conditions: What weight is given the surveys that the representatives of mass media use in soliciting advertisements? The prestige of the research people in the organization and outside might turn out to be more important than the substantive content of the research findings. Students intending to work on such problems can learn much from Wilensky's book on intellectuals in the labor movement, especially from his ingenious quantitative account of the degree of influence they have in various types of unions (62, chap. x).

Hierarchical status relations are of course involved in all this. If we do not insist on full specificity, we can include here two studies dealing with the general types of problems the businessman has to solve in his relations with his superiors and subordinates, respectively. The two efforts become especially interesting if viewed in conjunction. The Useems studied "social stress and resources among middle management men" by giving questionnaires to a thousand respondents so situated that they had at least two hierarchical levels below and two above them (61). Using something like Flanagan's critical incident technique (40), they explored eleven aspects of the jobs: whether they could use their abilities to the full, what kind of co-operation they got from others, etc. From the preliminary report I understand that they developed two scales for each area: one measuring the respondents' amount of involvement, and another measuring the amount of blockage encountered. Among the sources of stress singled out by the Useems are lack of co-operation by associates, too much or too little guidance by superiors, and insufficient information about what is going on in the company. They introduce the notion of "social resources," those factors which alleviate stress or prevent the rise of stress. They discuss "anticipatory learning, which occurs after the men entered the working world but in advance of occupying the particular statuses they now hold" (61, p. 84). This, of course, is an application of Merton's notion of anticipatory socialization (124). The Useems notice that the stresses diminish as a man moves up the hierarchical scale because he himself, as well as the men he meets, have become more adjusted to the environment of the organization and therefore their actions become more mutually predictable. The men learn to anticipate difficulties and to consider them more as manageable than as unavoidable "fate." The authors think that flexibility increases with time—though one has to wait for the statistical findings to decide whether this is not due to the fact that the Useems deal only with those persons who have successfully survived in their firms.

The middle-management people of the Useems are much concerned with their superiors. What, in turn, is their problem? A detailed description of "the executive system" in a single British factory by Elliot Jaques contains a section on "sources of stress in T-Group leadership" (46). "T-Group" refers to the pattern of relations between an executive and his immediate subordinates at various levels of the organization. Jaques singles out the anxieties that go with responsibilities; the unconscious ambivalence resulting from a desire to dominate which has to be repressed for the sake of work efficiency; the leader who has nobody to talk to and continually feels threatened by the potential power of his subordinates, which does not materialize, only because they in turn can not really form coalitions against him — for reasons closely linked with their stress as the Useems describe it.

A few sentences can not reproduce the broad range of stimulating ideas provided by both authors. At the same time they should suffice to show that more specific information would be needed if one wanted to know how generally and with what variations their observations are correct. Restricting the discussion to the boss, one may raise the following questions. How does an executive allocate his time? If many members of an organization make claims on the time of the executive, how does he decide whom to see? How does he appease those he cannot see? Does he distribute his attention evenly over a series of problems, or does he attend to the most urgent one, letting others accumulate until he feels vaguely that they have reached a danger point and require immediate attention? In the latter case, what sources of communication does he have for sensing danger points? Dahl and Lindblom have extended the term "sampling" to cover the various ways in which managers may inform themselves about the activities and problems of their subordinates (35, p. 65). But, even if a superior has the necessary information, how does he balance the needs of his subordinates for comfort or rational help against his tendency to follow those lines of his work which alleviate his own anxiety?[15]

The influence of the superior on his subordinates is part of the complex which, within the business world, is called "managerial development"—the training of junior executives. It seems that, in spite of efforts by the company to provide formal education, the young aspirant is primarily influenced by the particular character and practices of the man under whom he works (68). This would lead to the conclusion that training is a major duty for a senior man. He, however, gets his main reward from more visible performances and is therefore likely to neglect his role in educating juniors—however important he knows it to be for the company as a whole.[16] An additional problem is, of course, the dilemma of the man who is supposed to improve a potential competitor.

The last example has already introduced the notion of "visibility" which can be considered a third aspect of personal influence. Blau was one of the first to stress how greatly the performance of a staff is affected by the kind of records kept and brought to the attention of superiors (30). The idea serves to bring together a variety of case studies. Thus Granick tells about the difficulties experienced by the Russians in introducing "dispatching systems" into their factories to provide co-ordination between different departments. "The management could not have accomplished this without moving trained technical personnel from their old jobs. Almost certainly the plant would for a time have shown less success in meeting production orders," which are supposedly more visible to the central authority (43, p.

[15] Argyris, in a very perceptive case study, first describes the activities of a factory manager and then traces the effect he has on his subordinates (28).

[16] According to Samuel Stouffer, this is one of the most "sociological" of all business problems (personal communication). Further issues in training are dealt with by Allen (113), Andrews (114), and Nelson (125).

110 ft.). A similar experience is reported by Devons in a most instructive analysis of English aircraft production during the last war, in which he shows that one problem was to balance the production of airplane bodies and accessory parts (37, p. 83). Divisional plants tended to overproduce accessories which could be stored conveniently, while "the existence of airframes lying about unusable for want of some component was always a spectacular disaster, giving rise to innumerable inquiries and inquests instituted by highest authorities." The juxtaposition of such far-flung episodes raises the question of whether sociological concepts such as social visibility may not one day themselves become determinants of managerial activities.

To round out the picture, two studies are included in the Bibliography which describe how informal contacts between businessmen affected their reaction to control of prices (47) and raw materials (49) in wartime. Following my general scheme, the next section does not deal directly with specific motives but rather with the general dispositions likely to be related to them.

The "Motivation" of the Businessman[17]

In his review of the literature on the qualifications required by a business executive, Mandell points out that most of it is based on speculations, and he ends with the conclusion that "we do not know as yet which qualifications are most important in which situations, and which person will be most successful in a given job" (84). He summarizes current thinking with a checklist of relevant attributes that is conducive to empirical studies (84, p. 255). Anne Roe, in her exhaustive survey, found only three minor studies comparing test scores of business executives with those of other groups (89, p. 184).

Some inferences can be drawn from McClelland's test of achievement needs. It consists of showing the subject pictures of two or

---

[17] The material here covers the full variety of disposition concepts laid out in a preceding section. My original plan to locate each study and idea in its proper "cell" turned out to be irritating rather than helpful, but the reader who tries to do so himself may find it clarifying. I have attempted to adhere to a fairly consistent terminology.

three people in unstructured situations, having him guess what is going on, and then counting the number of references he makes to competitive situations or to ambitious goals (107). In an unpublished paper McClelland argues that his test will successfully single out business talent (83). He lists studies showing that students scoring high on the need for achievement prefer risky occupations of a business nature, that ethnic groups known for their business acumen score higher on these tests, and that countries where the stories told to children have a high "achievement content" have a higher rate of economic progress. The author proposes an interesting modification of aid to underdeveloped countries based on the idea of finding and developing people with high achievement-test scores.[18]

The quality signified by the phrase "tolerance of ambiguity" also calls for inquiry. The more difficult problems will more likely be referred to higher echelons. The ability to make decisions under such circumstances might well be correlated with one of the tests developed in the wake of Else Frenkel-Brunswik's paper on "Tolerance toward Ambiguity as a Personality Variable" (70). The handling of under-defined problems has, incidentally, found attention in another field— the sociology of medical education. Renée Fox's paper on "Training for Uncertainty" can be profitably read in the present context (69).[19]

In a way, Rosenberg has data bearing most directly on dispositions, because he compares the dispositions of Cornell College students who intend to go into business with their classmates who have other plans (91). (He refers to attitudes and values, although it is not quite clear how he distinguishes between the two kinds of items in his questionnaire.) That these prospective businessmen are less concerned with self-expression and more concerned with making money is not surprising; that they stand between engineers and social workers in regard to "people orientation" is less expected (91, chap. ii). But his data acquire high significance when he shows how frequently money-mak-

[18] The large group of McClelland's collaborators has never tested businessmen directly, but I understand they intend to.
[19] The recent "sharp increase in concern with the problem of creativity" has completely excluded businessmen as an object of investigation (93).

ing is seen as achieved through the use of questionable means rather than by the proverbial "hard work" (91, chap. viii). Rosenberg's wealth of data and subtlety of analysis can not be reproduced in brief; let me emphasize, however, that he has reinterviewed some of his students so that he can study what determines the stability of occupational choice, and he pays special attention to the "reluctant businessmen" students, who know they will have to go into business, although they do not like it and have characteristics disposing them to other choices (91, chap. ix).

Most of the available literature has to do with the motivation of the businessman as a generalized, driving, and time-spanning disposition that is inferred either as a functional requirement of the job, as a consequence of its exercise, or as a personal characteristic necessary for success in it. For a first orientation one finds sophisticated ideas in some articles published by *Fortune:* Klaw on the "entrepreneurial ego" (78), Luce on the "character of the businessman" (82), and Stryker on the "emotionally stable" executive (94). While these articles are often based on extensive collections of observations, the authors unfortunately do not tell enough about them to permit their conclusions to be evaluated.

The more conventional empirical studies show a surprising parallel to what in the consumer field we have met as motivation research, the product-consumer relation being replaced by the job-person relation. The relevant dispositions are brought to light by projective tests and detailed interviews; the "findings" are stimulating but unsupported generalizations strongly influenced by "depth psychology." Thus Warner and Abegglen focus on the fact that the successful businessman, particularly if he comes from the lower strata, has gone through many phases of "departure and arrival," moving from one job to the one next higher (95). His personal relations are therefore characterized by basic emotional coldness combined with an external ability to get along; and this in turn is traced to a childhood constellation with "negative feeling toward the mother as the figure who attempts to hold and control the son, and where the father seems in most cases to have been distant from the son" (95, p. 77). William E. Henry goes even further and claims that a "residual emotional tie [to the mother] seems contradictory to the necessary attitude of activity, progress and channeled aggression [and therefore accounts] systematically for difficulty in the business situations" (75). The repeated word "seems" is a substitute for a frank acknowledgment of the tremendous difficulty of working out an empirical test of such ideas and reinforces the parallel with the practices of commercial motivation research.

Even when a political scientist explores the "business mind," he is inclined to resort to what one might call high-level motivation research. In studying reactions to government regulations, Lane derives from a score of detailed interviews the businessman's need for deference and self-respect and his cathartic aggression when his ego is threatened by bureaucratic interference; the self-image of the businessman is repeatedly invoked (80). Lane's study contains a great deal of solid material from which he draws sound and important practical conclusions; only those parts of his compact report belong here which show how, for each level of action, "motivation research" develops. It is an effort to relate the specific feature of an "outside" object — a product, the government —to pertinent dispositions of actors by extremely tentative and as yet untestable procedures. I know of only one case in which precise measurement was made of a disposition—a frame of reference—within the context of a business situation: representatives of labor and management, involved in a dispute, looked at photographs of men who varied in their conventional attractiveness and who were alternately designated as labor leaders or as business executives (73). A tough-looking character was designated by labor leaders as "arrogant" if he was believed to a be a businessman and "energetic" if he was thought a labor leader. Inversely, the business people described him as "powerful-looking" in the former case and "crude" in the latter. All other combinations of looks, description, and judgment corresponded to the expectations suggested to the reader by this one example.

Historical and comparative studies of the role of the entrepreneur in economic development are providing an additional source for ideas on motivation. An extract from Redlich's survey of the pertinent literature on the diverse origins and variant forms of business leadership is characteristic:

The profit motive itself is but a historical category and is always coupled with other motives. Simply holding out the prospect of profit will hardly move an indigenous trader or money lender to become a modern industrialist or banker. But nationalism added to the urge for profit may suffice, as it did in Japan by 1870; and so may the desire to rise high in society, as in the same country by 1900. Indian conditions indicate that a specific family structure may prove favorable to the emergence of business leadership, and by some strange twist certain religious creeds may unexpectedly provide a stimulus, as in Western countries in the case of the Puritans [88, p. 187].

This statement obviously deals with the kind of motivation that is supposedly often found among businessmen or that may be assessed as a motive in empirical studies of their career choices. But it implicitly challenges the idea that this disposition is identical with the narrow goal of making money, something I doubt has ever been seriously claimed even by theoretical economists. Instead it points to the "coupling" of several "motives." There is no difficulty in assuming that a variety of dispositions may be characteristic of businessmen and correlated with success in their pursuits. If one were to analyze specific decisions, a number of such dispositions could, no doubt, be assessed as motives, just as a consumer could be influenced by, say, a sequence of media in the course of a purchase. Finally, some of these effective dispositions could be more socially required and rewarded than others — the role of "values" in this sense is the main theme of Parsons' "motivation of economic activities" (87).

Our interest in this broad approach to the entrepreneur[20] lies in the fact that it suggests some empirical studies and throws new light on some theoretical ideas. If the attitudes, favorable traits, and successful combinations of goals of businessmen have varied in different his-

---

[20] It is best represented by the journal *Explorations in Entrepreneurial History*, which has many contributions of sociological interest and, as a matter of fact, probably represents the closest alliance between history and sociology. I use the terms "businessman," "manager," and "entrepreneur" interchangeably, although in other contexts distinctions would be relevant.

torical situations, then there should be variations of the same kind in the various sectors of the complex map of modern American business. It is quite likely that various types of industries, businesses of different sizes, and more or less centralized organizations require various kinds of leadership. In differing phases of the development of an industry, different types of background are more likely to lead to top positions. When the company is young, its president is apt to have had training as an engineer; as production problems are solved, the sales executive is likely to come to the top; as government plays an increasingly large role in business affairs, the lawyer receives his chance for advancement. Each shift should bring with it new problems in the relations between top executives, on the one hand, and different technical and social aspects of the organization, on the other. All through recent history there has been a steady increase in the number of variables a business-man has had to take into account. Historical and comparative studies will sensitize us to the way various business situations may differently affect the type of men likely to be successful. For specific leads one might consult the history of business by Gras (72) or the anthro-pological survey by Belshaw (65).

From the theoretical side the modern comparative approach repre-sents an interesting development, or even, inversion of Max Weber's ideas. He investigated the religious ideas in the Orient that inhibited the development of a capitalistic economy; the new problem is to see what other ideologies contribute to economic development or hinder it. Recent history has raised the problem, whether the Puritan ethic and further economic growth are not contradictory and whether new types of "motivations" instead have become a consequence and a re-quirement of modern technological and organizational change.

In this country the graduate school of business increasingly supplies personnel for large corporations and a period of study in one of these schools becomes part of the independent businessman's biography. Some of these schools' educational problems can be gleaned from a symposium on professional education organized by the Carnegie Corporation (67). The function of sociology in all professional train-ing, which Young has emphasized, deserves special inquiry in the case of business education because its goals and strategies are less firmly agreed upon than in the professions (96). A comprehensive study extending over several years should be designed along the lines of the study of medical schools currently being undertaken by Merton and his associates. They focus on the attitudes which these schools engender and on the ways in which they socialize students for their future role (86).

The Businessman's Role

A complex social activity is described as a "role" when attention focuses on customary ways of discharging it, on the expectations that various social groups have about it, and on the links it has with other aspects of the social fabric. I can not even begin to apply seriously the rapidly developing theory of roles to the growing diversity of business activities, but for illustrative purposes, however, I shall single out a few characteristic problems which might find their place in a future systematic approach. These will deal with *a*) a change in performance of roles; *b*) some tensions arising from intrinsic requirements of roles; *c*) conflicting expectations; and *d*) an issue derived from the businessman's role in the economic system viewed as an institution.

a) The function of the entrepreneur has been discussed in a practically inexhaustible literature within which three main emphases can be distinguished. Administrative theory has stressed the function of the businessman in *co-ordinating* the different parts of the business organization, and considerable descriptive material is available. Economic theorists have discussed the willingness of businessmen to *take risks,* mainly in connection with theories of profit or, more generally, the allocation of rewards. Little empirical research seems to have resulted from this approach; the recent mathematical work on "decision under risk" appears to have little relation to the classical form of the discussion.

Economic historians have stressed the innovating elements in the role of the businessman. The sociologist has something to say about this point because of changes which have come about in recent times.

A generation or so ago a great premium was placed on the ability to think of new products, to anticipate organizational difficulties in time, and to be farsighted enough to predict changes in market conditions. Today each of these matters is the object of continuous study, often by commercial groups specializing in these services. As a result, the executives of big corporations are besieged today by representatives of agencies which have studied their needs for development of products, which—in the hope of obtaining a new client—have invested in a human relations study of the firm, and which would include in their package one of the many existing market forecasts. Previously the innovating vision was crucial, but what matters today is the ability to keep track of all these developments, to make the best purchase in their market, or to organize research and development divisions within the company.

This shift in the way the businessman discharges his innovating function has led to several new lines of social inquiry. For one, industrial research organizations have themselves been studied.[21] But, strangely enough, sociologists have neglected the social research work that is going on in industrial firms, in advertising agencies, and in university institutes conducting research for business firms. The latter provide an especially interesting problem because they themselves represent a real innovation within the academic structure and undoubtedly have begun to affect practices of sociological training. Second, the process of change itself has received detailed attention, especially in the case-study tradition of the Harvard Business School (116, 127, 128). But here, again, only one part of the picture has been examined. Most of this material focuses on the consequences a change might have for an organization, a concern which is understandable from a "human relations" point of view. But the sources of the change and the processes by which it came about have been neglected.

b) Another set of problems arises when the requirements of an occupation are in conflict with the dispositions of people in it, whether these are personal attitudes or culturally induced values. During the

---

[21] For an informative summary see Pelz (56).

McCarthy period, for instance, many officers of the broadcasting companies experienced great tension between their personal convictions and the policy of their organizations to blacklist performers at the slightest suspicion of left-wing association. Jahoda reports in detail the reactions of these men of liberal backgrounds who were charged with carrying out the company's policies (77). One knows only from hearsay about the problem of those of the ten thousand editors of industrial house organs who are by definition agents of their firms but whose journalistic training exalts an unbiased presentation of facts. Similarly, the country store owner finds himself torn between the claims of manufacturers and the interests of customers, who are also his neighbors. So, too, Krugman has reported some evidence of the conflicts experienced by insurance salesmen who must continuously invade the privacy of other people and whose success therefore depends upon the violation of a major social taboo (79).[22]

An especially interesting case in point is the small businessman, whom Mayer has studied in some detail (85). While in previous examples motivations conflicted with occupational realities, in this instance they degenerate in an occupational vacuum. The desire to have a business of one's own is still very widespread, especially among the working class, but the chances of continuing success are slim. This affects the nature of the desire itself. Only half of the people who would like to go into a business of their own think that this would be realistically possible; when asked whether hard work is likely to help toward this goal, many feel that this is so, in general, but express great skepticism about their own success. The whole situation is "likely to mislead and misdirect the aspirations of millions of people who cherish an outdated concept of business opportunity, resulting inevitably in frustration." Mayer emphasizes that little is known about "entries and discontinuances, because individual cases have not yet been studied in sufficient number or detail." Special attention might

[22] Insurance salesmen, though employees of their companies, need the skills of an independent entrepreneur. Data about their work are available in the Life Insurance Agency Management Association's continuing industry-wide studies; the material that it publishes in its yearly *Digest* deserves sociological reanalysis.

be given to marginal cases like automobile dealers, who, while in a business of their own, are dependent upon the car manufacturers (90).

c) We come next to the effects of conflicting reference groups.[23] The salaried professional whose loyalty is split between his company and his profession is by now a well-established object of sociological concern. To him we might add the businessman who, after a stint in Washington, feels uneasy about his local trade association because he can not unreservedly condemn government interference in business affairs, or the broadcaster whose educated friends blame him for the lowbrow programs he permits on his network.

Inversely, business groups are often the objects of divergent expectations. The mass media provide a good case in point. Parents and teachers expect them to fulfill a cultural and educational mission, while the majority of the audience just want to be entertained. The criticism which liberal intellectuals direct against the industry is especially bitter because they feel that they really have provided the masses with the leisure and the money which now are dissipated (81). The fervor of a few decades ago to enact social legislation or curb monopolies seems today to be channeled into deploring the low level of mass culture. An analysis of the controversy would provide a distinct contribution to Hughes's recent theory of "mandates and licenses" (76). According to him, every occupation has the right to "carry out certain activities rather different from those of other people" and at the same time the duty "to define—not merely for themselves but for others as well—proper conduct with respect to the matters concerned in their work." The commercial broadcaster feels that he is entitled to act according to business principles in an area in which parents and teachers have traditionally set the standards. Both sides exclude the government as an arbiter because in the communication of ideas—in contrast to physical communication—it is not supposed to be competent. The result is an uneasy equilibrium that some writers, such as Laski in his discussion of mass media, have

---

[23] Cf. reference above to the influence of the research men in business organizations upon managerial decisions.

admired as "the self-correcting mechanism" of the American system (122), while others, such as van den Haag, have deplored because it "impoverishes life without leading to contentment" (131).

Other types of economic activities are "affected by public interest" in a more or less intangible way, and thus make for complexities in the role of the businessman. Large scale housing is certainly one. The claimed fiduciary role of the banker is probably another, and Argyris has shown some of the consequences this has for the selection of its personnel and the social relations among them (63). What Hughes has described as the "sociology of work," however, deserves a more extensive application to business occupations than it has found so far. Situations tangential to a businessman's main work should not be excluded from consideration. How does he behave when he is on the board of a hospital or is a trustee of a university? Does he follow his usual pattern, or does he look for compensatory satisfactions? At this moment many philanthropic organizations resound with the conflict between those who favor separate fund-raising and those who prefer a central community chest; in this debate it turns out that some board members believe that competition, as in business, is most productive here. Others look for a different kind of atmosphere when they turn to civic activities. This is the type of occasion which ought to be rich in research opportunities.

d) By extending somewhat the notion of role, one can, finally, raise this question: What restrictions face the American businessman today, and how, on the other hand, is his situation facilitated? Let us approach the matter indirectly.

There exists some literature comparing European and American managerial practices (74, 29). The observers generally agree that remnants of a "feudal social structure" in Europe fetter the full development of efficiency of the kind found in the United States. Recruitment to top positions is affected by family connections and restricted to a small upper stratum. As a consequence, even in larger corporations staff work is less extensive, and the top executives, forced to undertake activities themselves, feel reluctant to expand their enterprises. At the same time it is expected that economic success will be accompanied by more general cultural activities. Thus "the social order in France has in some measure undervalued the very prizes and penalties that have urged on the capitalistic process" (92, p. 16). By contrast, in the United States the historical circumstances led to a general value system and to recruitment policies that were favorable to rapid industrialization and economic growth.

Now let us assume for the moment that a historian two hundred years hence again asks what relation there was between social structure and economic institutions here in the mid-twentieth century. He will first notice that American businessmen began then to find themselves handicapped by the remnants of an older social structure. Because "free enterprise" had made the country great, they believed the trend toward a national organization of economic resources to be a threat to their interests. Just as feudal ghosts kept the European businessman from developing full administrative efficiency, so the ghosts of an earlier capitalism led his American counterpart a few decades later to waste resources in trying to block social legislation, in accepting government regulations only under duress, and in supporting political parties which had lost their own grass roots. This resistance was not, however, universal. In some parts of the business community the new social values had "become so widely accepted that the costs of achieving them had become part of the normal cost of business and therefore recoverable through price" (66, p. 40). The historian would want to know more precisely in which groups and by what steps this "new look" of business developed. He will blame today's sociologists for not providing him with better studies of this issue. And he will be irked by a strange question that was raised at the time: Do the so-called progressive business leaders really mean it? Who asked whether Weber's early capitalists "really meant" their fusion of business and religion? But after some thought the future historian will realize that his criticism is facile, because he will know how things turned out. Today, however, we do not know whether the managerial revolution will lead to a new postcapitalistic economy or to a perversion of democracy by a politico-economic power elite. Appropriately, these reflections are interrupted on a note of doubt.

Selected Bibliography

A. CONSUMER BEHAVIOR

1. AMERICAN MARKETING ASSOCIATION. *The Technique of Market Research.* New York, McGraw-Hill Book Co., 1936.
2. BAUER, RAYMOND. "The Communicator and the Audience," *Conflict Resolution,* II (March, 1958), 67–77.
3. BERELSON, BERNARD, PAUL F. LAZARSFELD, and WILLIAM McPHEE. *Voting.* Chicago, University of Chicago Press, 1954.
4. BILKEY, WARREN J. "A Psychological Approach to Consumer Behavior Analysis," *Journal of Marketing,* XVIII (July, 1953), 18–25.
5. ———. "Psychic Tensions and Purchasing Behavior," *Journal of Social Psychology,* XLI (1955), 247–57.
6. BOURNE, FRANCIS S. "Group Influences in Marketing and Public Relations," in RENSIS LIKERT and SAMUEL P. HAYES (eds.), *Some Applications of Behavioral Research,* pp. 205–57. ("Science and Society Series.") New York, UNESCO, 1957.
7. CAPLOW, THEODORE, and J. RAYMOND. "Factors Influencing the Selection of Pharmaceutical Products," *Journal of Marketing,* XIX (July, 1954), 18–23.
8. COLEMAN, JAMES, ELIHU KATZ, and HERBERT MENZEL. "The Diffusion of an Innovation among Physicians," *Sociometry,* XX (December, 1957), 253–70.
9. DUESENBERRY, JAMES S. *Income, Savings and the Theory of Consumer Behavior.* Cambridge, Mass., Harvard University Press, 1952.
10. ERDELYI, MICHAEL. "The Relation between 'Radio Plugs' and Sheet Sales of Popular Music," *Journal of Applied Psychology,* XXIV (December, 1940), 696–702.
11. ETZIONI, AMITAI. "Administration and the Consumer," *Administrative Science Quarterly,* III (September, 1958), 251–64.
12. GARDNER, BURLEIGH, and SIDNEY LEVY. "The Product and the Brand," *Harvard Business Review,* XXXIII (March–April, 1955), 33–39.
13. GARDNER, BURLEIGH, and LEE RAINWATER. "The Mass Image of Big Business," *Harvard Business Review,* XXXIII (November–December, 1955), 61–66.
14. HAIRE, MASON. "Projective Techniques in Market Research," *Journal of Marketing,* XIV (April, 1950), 649–56.
15. HERZOG, HERTA. "What Do We Really Know about Daytime Serial Listeners," in P. F. LAZARSFELD and F. STANTON (eds.), *Radio Research, 1942–1943,* pp. 3–33. New York, Duell, Sloan and Pearce, 1944.
16. KATONA, GEORGE. "The Effect of Income Changes on the Rate of Savings,"

in P. F. Lazarsfeld and Morris Rosenberg (eds.), *The Language of Social Research*, pp. 184–94. Glencoe, Ill., The Free Press, 1955.

17. Katona, George, and Eva Mueller. "A Study of Purchase Decisions," in L. H. Clark (ed.), *Consumer Behavior*, pp. 30–87. New York, New York University Press, 1954.

18. Katz, Elihu, and P. F. Lazarsfeld. *Personal Influence*. Glencoe, Ill., The Free Press, 1955.

19. Lazarsfeld, Paul F. "Progress and Fad in Motivation Research," in *Social Science for Industry Motivation: Proceedings of Stanford Research Institute, Third Annual Seminar*, pp. 11–23. Menlo Park, Calif., Stanford Research Institute, 1955. (Also Publication A182, Columbia University, Bureau of Applied Social Research [New York, 1955].)

20. Lazarsfeld, Paul F., and Patricia L. Kendall. *Radio Listening in America*. New York, Prentice-Hall, Inc. 1948.

21. Lynd, Robert S. "The People as Consumers," in *Recent Social Trends*, pp. 857–911. New York, McGraw-Hill Book Co., 1933.

22. Menzel, Herbert, and Elihu Katz. "Social Relations and Innovations in the Medical Profession," *Public Opinion Quarterly*, xix (Winter, 1955–56), 337–57.

23. Newman, Joseph. *Motivation Research and Marketing Management*. Boston, Harvard Graduate School of Business Administration, Division of Research, 1957.

24. Roshwalb, Irving. "The Voting Studies and Consumer Behavior," in Eugene Burdick and Arthur J. Brodbeck (eds.), *American Voting Behavior*, pp. 150–61. Glencoe, Ill., The Free Press, 1959.

25. Smith, Elias, and Edward A. Suchman. "Do People Know Why They Buy?" in P. F. Lazarsfeld and M. Rosenberg (eds.), *The Language of Social Research*, pp. 404–11. Glencoe, Ill., The Free Press, 1955.

26. Smith, George Horsley. *Motivation Research in Advertising and Marketing*. New York, McGraw-Hill Book Co., 1954.

27. Stone, Gregory. "City Shoppers and Urban Identification," *American Journal of Sociology*, lx (July, 1954), 36–45.

B. MANAGERIAL ACTIVITIES

28. Argyris, Chris. *Executive Leadership*. New York, Harper and Bros., 1953.

29. Barton, Allen. "Sociological and Psychological Problems of Economic Planning in Norway." Unpublished doctoral dissertation, Columbia University, 1957.

30. Blau, Peter. *The Dynamics of Bureaucracy*. Chicago, University of Chicago Press, 1955.

31. CARLSON, SUNE. *Executive Behavior*. Stockholm: Strombergs Aktiebolag, 1951.
32. COPELAND, MELVIN T. *The Executive at Work*. Cambridge, Mass., Harvard University Press, 1951.
33. CRANDELL, RUTH. "Autobiographies of Businessmen," *Explorations in Entrepreneurial History*, x (April, 1958), 154–61.
34. CYERT, RICHARD M., HERBERT A. SIMON, and DONALD B. TROW, "Observation of a Business Decision," *Journal of Business of the University of Chicago*, XXIX (October, 1956), 237–48.
35. DAHL, ROBERT A., and CHARLES LINDBLOM. *Politics, Economics, and Welfare*. New York, Harper and Bros., 1953.
36. DE SOLA POOL, I., SUZANNE KELLER, and RAYMOND BAUER. "The Influence of Foreign Travel on Political Attitudes of American Businessmen," *Public Opinion Quarterly*, xx (Spring, 1956), 161–75.
37. DEVONS, ELY. *Planning in Practice*. Cambridge, Cambridge University Press, 1950.
38. DONHAM, PAUL, et al. "The Growth Problems of Smaller Businessmen," in D. H. FENN (ed.), *Management in a Rapidly Changing Economy*, pp. 218–47. New York, McGraw-Hill Book Co., 1958.
39. ELLIS, PAUL WARREN. *Effects of Taxes upon Corporate Policy*. New York, National Industry Conference Board, 1943.
40. FLANAGAN, JOHN C. "The Critical Incident Technique in Defining Job Requirements," in M. J. DOOHER and E. MARTING (eds.), *Selection of Management Personnel*, I, 366–80. New York, American Management Association, 1957.
41. GORT, MICHAEL. "The Planning of Investment: A Study of Capital Budgeting in the Electric Power Industry, I" *Journal of Business of the University of Chicago*, XXIV (April, 1951), 79–95.
42. GOULDNER, ALVIN W. "Organizational Analysis," in R. K. MERTON, L. BROOM, and L. COTTRELL (eds.), *Sociology Today*, pp. 400–428. New York, Basic Books, 1959.
43. GRANICK, D. *Management of the Industrial Firm in the U.S.S.R.* New York, Columbia University Press, 1953.
44. GUETZKOW, HAROLD. "An Exploratory Empirical Study of the Role of Conflict in Decision-making Conferences," *International Social Science Bulletin*, v (1953), 286–300.
45. GUETZKOW, HAROLD, and JOHN GYR. "An Analysis of Conflict in Decision-making Groups," *Human Relations*, VII (1954), 367–81.
46. JAQUES, ELLIOT. *The Changing Culture of a Factory*. New York, Dryden Press, 1952.

47. KATONA, GEORGE. *Price Control and Business*. Bloomington, Ill., Principia Press, 1954.
48. KATONA, GEORGE, and JAMES MORGAN. "The Quantitative Study of Factors Determining Business Decisions," *Quarterly Journal of Economics*, LXVI (February, 1952), 67–90.
49. KRIESBERG, LOUIS. "Occupational Controls among Steel Distributors," *American Journal of Sociology*, LXI (November, 1955), 203–12.
50. McGREGOR, D. "The Staff Function in Human Relationships," *Journal of Social Issues*, IV (1948), 5–22.
51. MACHLUP, FRITZ. "Marginal Analysis and Empirical Research," *American Economic Review*, XXXVI (September, 1946), 519–54.
52. MANN, FLOYD C. "Studying and Creating Change: A Means to Understanding Social Organization," in CONRAD ARENSBERG et al. (eds.), *Research in Industrial Human Relations*, pp. 146–67. New York, Harper and Bros., 1957.
53. MARCH, JAMES G., and HERBERT A. SIMON. *Organizations*. New York, John Wiley and Sons, 1958.
54. MODIGLIANI, FRANCO, and F. E. BALDERSTON. "Economic Analysis and Forecasting: Recent Developments in the Use of Panel and Other Survey Techniques," in EUGENE BURDICK and A. J. BRODBECK (eds.), *American Voting Behavior*, pp. 372–98. Glencoe, Ill., The Free Press, 1959.
55. OXENFELDT, ALFRED. *Industrial Pricing and Marketing Practices*. New York, Prentice-Hall, Inc., 1951.
56. PELZ, DONALD C. "Some Social Factors Related to Performance in a Research Organization," *Administrative Science Quarterly*, I (1956), 310–32.
57. PETER, HOLLIS W. "Human Factors in Research Administration," in RENSIS LIKERT and SAMUEL P. HAYES (eds.), *Some Applications of Behavioral Research*, 124–59. ("Science and Society Series.") New York, UNESCO, 1957.
58. ROSENMAN, SAMUEL I. *Working with Roosevelt*. New York, Harper and Bros., 1952.
59. SIMON, HERBERT A. *Models of Man*. New York, John Wiley and Sons, 1957.
60. STOGDILL, RALPH M., and CARROL L. SHARTLE. *Methods in the Study of Administrative Leadership*. (Bureau of Business Research Monograph No. 80.) Columbus, Ohio State University, 1955.
61. USEEM, JOHN and RUTH. "Social Stress and Resources among Middle Management," in E. GARTLEY JACO (ed.), *Patients, Physicians and Illness*, pp. 74–91. Glencoe, Ill., The Free Press, 1958.
62. WILENSKY, HAROLD. *Intellectuals in Labor Unions*. Glencoe, Ill., The Free Press, 1956.

C. MOTIVATION AND ROLE OF BUSINESSMEN

63. ARGYRIS, CHRIS. *Organization of a Bank.* New Haven, Conn., Yale University Labor and Management Center, 1954.

64. BARNARD, CHESTER L. *Functions of the Executive.* Cambridge, Mass., Harvard University Press, 1938.

65. BELSHAW, CYRIL S. "The Cultural Milieu of the Entrepreneur: A Critical Essay," in *Explorations in Entrepreneurial History,* VII (February, 1955), 146–63.

66. BOWEN, HOWARD R. *The Business Enterprise as a Subject for Research.* (Social Science Research Council Pamphlet No. 11.) New York, 1957.

67. CARNEGIE CORPORATION. "Education for Professional Responsibility," in *Proceedings of an Inter-professions Conference, Buck Hills Falls, Pennsylvania, 1948.* Pittsburgh, Carnegie Press, 1948.

68. FLEISHMAN, E. A., *et al. Leadership and Supervision in Industry.* Columbus, Ohio State University Personnel Research Board, 1955.

69. FOX, RENÉE. "Training for Uncertainty," in ROBERT K. MERTON, GEORGE G. READER, and PATRICIA L. KENDALL (eds.), *The Student-Physician,* pp. 207–41. Cambridge, Mass., Harvard University Press, 1957.

70. FRENKEL-BRUNSWIK, ELSE. "Tolerance toward Ambiguity as a Personality Variable," *American Psychologist,* III (1948), 268.

71. GORDON, ROBERT A. *Business Leadership in the Large Corporation.* Washington, D.C., Brookings Institution, 1945.

72. GRAS, N. S. B. *Business and Capitalism.* New York, F. S. Crofts Co., 1947.

73. HAIRE, MASON. "Role Perceptions in Labor-Management Relations: An Experimental Approach," *Industrial and Labor Relations Review,* VIII (January, 1955), 204–16. (Also University of California Institute of Industrial Relations Reprint No. 66 [Berkeley, 1955].)

74. HARBISON, F. H., and E. W. BURGESS. "Modern Management in Western Europe," *American Journal of Sociology,* LX (July, 1954), 15–23.

75. HENRY, WILLIAM E. "The Business Executive: The Psychodynamics of a Social Role," *American Journal of Sociology,* LIV (January, 1949), 286–91.

76. HUGHES, EVERETT C. *Men and Their Work.* Glencoe, Ill., The Free Press, 1958.

77. JAHODA, MARIE. "Anti-communism and Employment Policies in Radio and Television," in JOHN COGLEY (ed.), *Report on Blacklisting* II: *Radio and Television,* pp. 221–81. New York, Fund for the Republic, 1956.

78. KLAW, SPENCER. "The Entrepreneurial Ego," *Fortune,* LIV (August, 1956), 100.

79. KRUGMAN, HERBERT E. "Salesmen in Conflict: A Challenge to Marketing," *Journal of Marketing,* XXIII (July, 1958), 59–61.

80. LANE, ROBERT E. *The Regulation of Businessmen.* New Haven, Conn., Yale University Press, 1954.

81. LAZARSFELD, PAUL F. "Role of Criticism in the Management of Mass Communications," in W. SCHRAMM (ed.), *Communications in Modern Society*, pp. 187–203. Urbana, University of Illinois Press, 1948.

82. LUCE, HENRY R. "The Character of the Businessman," *Fortune*, LVI (August, 1957), 108.

83. McCLELLAND, DAVID C. "Community Development and the Nature of Human Motivation." (Paper delivered at MIT Center for International Studies, Conference on Community Development.)

84. MANDELL, MILTON M. "The Selection of Executives," in M. J. DOOHER and E. MARTING (eds.), *Selection of Management Personnel*, I, 187–320. New York, American Management Association, 1957.

85. MAYER, KURT. "Business Enterprise: Traditional Symbol of Opportunity," *British Journal of Sociology*, IV (June, 1953), 160–80.

86. MERTON, ROBERT K., "Some Preliminaries to a Sociology of Medical Education," in ROBERT K. MERTON, GEORGE G. READER, and PATRICIA L. KENDALL (eds.), *The Student-Physician* pp. 3–79. Cambridge, Mass., Harvard University Press, 1957.

87. PARSONS, TALCOTT. "The Motivation of Economic Activities," *Essays in Sociological Theory*, pp. 200–217. Glencoe, Ill., The Free Press, 1949.

88. REDLICH, FRITZ. "Business Leadership: Diverse Origins and Variant Forms," *Economic Development and Cultural Change*, VI (April, 1958), 177–90.

89. ROE, ANNE. *The Psychology of Occupations.* New York, John Wiley and Sons, 1956.

90. ROGERS, DAVID. "The Automobile Dealer." Unpublished doctoral dissertation, Harvard University, 1959.

91. ROSENBERG, MORRIS. *Occupations and Values.* Glencoe, Ill., The Free Press, 1957.

92. SAWYER, JOHN E. "France and the United States," in WILLIAM MILLER (ed.), *Men in Business*, pp. 7–22. Cambridge, Mass., Harvard University Press, 1952.

93. STEIN, MORRIS I., *et al.* "Creativity and/or Success: A Study in Value Conflict," in *Second University of Utah Conference on the Identification of Creative Scientific Talent*, pp. 201–32. Salt Lake City, University of Utah Press, 1958.

94. STRYKER, PERRIN. "What Makes an 'Emotionally Stable' Executive?" *Fortune*, LVIII (July, 1958), 116.

95. WARNER, W. LLOYD, and JAMES C. ABEGGLEN. *Big Business Leaders in America.* New York, Harper and Bros., 1955.

96. YOUNG, DONALD. "Sociology and the Practicing Professions," *American Sociological Review,* xx (December, 1955), 641–47.

D. THE ANALYSIS OF ACTION: THEORY AND TECHNIQUE

97. ALLPORT, GORDON. "Attitudes," in CARL MURCHISON (ed.), *Handbook of Social Psychology,* pp. 798–844. Worcester, Mass., Clark University Press, 1935.

98. KADUSHIN, CHARLES. "Individual Decisions To Undertake Psychotherapy," *Administrative Science Quarterly,* III (December, 1958), 379–411.

99. KATONA, GEORGE. "Comments," in HOWARD R. BOWEN, *The Business Enterprise as a Subject for Research,* p. 40. (Social Science Research Council Pamphlet No. 11.) New York, 1957.

100. KLUCKHOHN, CLYDE. "Values and Value Orientations in the Theory of Action," in TALCOTT PARSONS and E. A. SHILS (eds.), *Toward a General Theory of Action,* pp. 388–433. Cambridge, Mass., Harvard University Press, 1951.

101. LAZARSFELD, PAUL F. "Evaluating the Effectiveness of Advertising in Direct Interviews," in PAUL F. LAZARSFELD and MORRIS ROSENBERG (eds.), *The Language of Social Research,* 411–19. Glencoe, Ill., The Free Press, 1955.

102. ———. "Interpretation of Statistical Relations as a Research Operation," *ibid.,* pp. 115–24.

103. ———. "Some Historical Notes on the Study of Action." (Paper to be included in a forthcoming volume on "The Empirical Study of Short-Range Change.")

104. LAZARSFELD, PAUL F. and ROBERT K. MERTON. "Friendship as Social Process," in M. BERGER, T. ABEL, and C. H. PAGE (eds.), *Freedom and Control in Modern Society,* pp. 18–66. New York, D. Van Nostrand and Co., 1954.

105. LAZARSFELD, PAUL F., and MORRIS ROSENBERG. *The Language of Social Research,* Introduction to Section v, pp. 387–91. Glencoe, Ill., The Free Press, 1955.

106. LIPSET, SEYMOUR M., *et al.* "The Psychology of Voting," in GARDNER LINDZEY (ed.), *Handbook of Social Psychology,* II, 1150 ff. Cambridge, Mass., Addison-Wesley Press, 1954.

107. McCLELLAND, D. C., J. W. ATKINSON, and E. L. LOWELL. *The Achievement Motive.* New York, Appleton-Century-Crofts, 1953.

108. PARSONS, TALCOTT. *The Structure of Social Action.* New York, McGraw-Hill Book Co., 1937.

109. ROSSI, PETER. *Why Families Move.* Glencoe, Ill., The Free Press, 1955.

110. TOLMAN, EDWARD C. "A Psychological Model," in TALCOTT PARSONS and

E. A. SHILS (eds.), *Toward A General Theory of Action*, pp. 279–361. Cambridge, Mass., Harvard University Press, 1951.

111. WEBER, MAX. *The Methodology of the Social Sciences*, trans. E. A. SHILS and H. A. FINCH. Glencoe, Ill., The Free Press, 1949.

112. ZEISEL, HANS. *Say it with Figures*. 4th ed. New York, Harper and Bros., 1957.

E. GENERAL BACKGROUND

113. ALLEN, LOUIS A. "Does Management Development Develop Managers?" *Personnel*, XXXIV (September–October, 1957), 18–25.

114. ANDREWS, KENNETH R. "Is Management Training Effective?" *Harvard Business Review*, XXXV, No. 1 (January–February, 1957), 85–94; *ibid.*, No. 2 (March–April, 1957), 63–72.

115. ARENSBERG, CONRAD M., and GEOFFREY TOOTELL. "Plant Sociology: Real Discoveries and New Problems," in M. KOMAROVSKY (ed.), *Common Frontiers of the Social Sciences*, pp. 310–37. Glencoe, Ill., The Free Press, 1957.

116. CRAIG, H. F. *Administering a Conversion to Electronic Accounting*. Boston, Harvard University Graduate School of Business Administration, Division of Research, 1952.

117. DIAMOND, SIGMUND. *The Reputation of the American Businessman*. Cambridge, Mass., Harvard University Press, 1955.

118. GALBRAITH, J. K. *The Affluent Society*. Boston, Houghton Mifflin Co., 1958.

119. GOMBERG, WILLIAM. "The Use of Psychology in Industry: A Trade Union Point of View," *Management Science*, III (July, 1957), 348–70.

120. KERR, CLARK, and LLOYD H. FISHER. "Plant Sociology: The Elite and the Aborigine," in M. KOMAROVSKY (ed.), *Common Frontiers of the Social Sciences*, pp. 281–309. Glencoe, Ill., The Free Press, 1957.

121. KORNHAUSER, ARTHUR. "Power Relationships and the Role of the Social Scientist," in ARTHUR KORNHAUSER (ed.), *Problems of Power in American Democracy*, pp. 184–217. Detroit, Wayne State University Press, 1957.

122. LASKI, HAROLD J. *The American Democracy*. New York, Viking Press, 1948.

123. LEKACHMAN, ROBERT. "The Non-economic Assumptions of John Maynard Keynes," in M. KOMAROVSKY (ed.), *Common Frontiers of the Social Sciences*, pp. 338–57. Glencoe, Ill., The Free Press, 1957.

124. MERTON, ROBERT K. *Social Theory and Social Structure*. Rev. ed. Glencoe, Ill., The Free Press, 1957.

125. NELSON, CHARLES A. "The Liberal Arts in Management," *Harvard Business Review*, XXXVI (May–June, 1958), 91–99.

126. PAPANDREOU, ANDREAS. "Some Problems in the Theory of the Firm," in B. F. HALEY (ed.), *A Survey of Contemporary Economics*, II, 183–219. Chicago, Richard D. Irwin, Inc., 1952.

127. RICHARDSON, F. L., and C. R. WALKER. *Human Relations in an Expanding Company.* New Haven, Conn., Yale University Labor and Management Center, 1948.

128. RONKEN, H. O., and P. R. LAWRENCE. *Administering Change.* Boston, Harvard University Graduate School of Business Administration, Division of Research, 1952.

129. SAYLES, LEONARD R., and GEORGE STRAUSS. *The Local Union.* New York, Harper and Bros. 1953.

130. SELZNICK, PHILIP. *Leadership in Administration.* Evanston, Ill., Row, Peterson and Co., 1957.

131. VAN DEN HAAG, ERNEST. "Of Happiness and Despair We Have No Measure," in B. ROSENBERG and D. M. WHITE (eds.), *Mass Culture,* pp. 504–36. Glencoe, Ill., The Free Press, 1957.

132. VICKREY, WILLIAM S. "A Note on Micro and Macroeconomics," in M. KOMAROVSKY (ed.), *Common Frontiers of the Social Sciences,* pp. 376–82. Glencoe, Ill., The Free Press, 1957.

133. WILENSKY, HAROLD. "Human Relations in the Workplace: An Appraisal of Some Recent Research," in C. ARENSBERG *et al.* (eds.), *Research in Industrial Human Relations,* pp. 25–50. New York, Harper and Bros., 1957.

An Annotated Bibliography

The following bibliography has been jointly selected by the authors to give the interested reader a broad view of the contributions of the social science disciplines to the study of business. Economic works are not included since most students of business are already familiar with them. In most cases articles or short essays have been omitted, though a few of a survey nature are included. The bibliography is not intended as a guide to all the important literature on the subject, but merely as an introduction to some of the more important materials.

ARGYRIS, CHRIS. *Personality and Organization*. New York, Harper and Bros., 1957. The sharpest statement of the conflict between the satisfaction of individual goals and organizational objectives. A psychological analysis of the characteristics of humans which leads to this end.

BARNARD, CHESTER I. *The Functions of the Executive*. Cambridge, Mass., Harvard University Press, 1938. A theoretical work by a successful executive. The book has had a seminal influence on administrative theory and has now achieved the status of a minor classic in the study of administration.

BEARD, MIRIAM. *A History of the Businessman*. New York, The Macmillan Co., 1938. An historical survey covering the activities, social and political position, and influences of the man of business from the earliest times to the present day.

BENDIX, REINHARD, and S. M. LIPSET (eds.). *Class, Status, and Power*. Glencoe, Ill., The Free Press, 1953. A collection of papers by about seventy authors. Contains empirical study of class differences as well as theoretical discussion on the nature of classes and their role in society.

BLAU, PETER. *Bureaucracy in Modern Society*. New York, Random House, 1956. Gives an idea of the way sociologists study business as well as government organizations. Includes interesting findings from the author's own studies.

BOWEN, HOWARD R. *The Business Enterprise as a Subject for Research*. Social Science Research Council, Pamphlet No. 11, 1957. A first attempt to lay out the field of business research in a systematic way. Raises interesting questions and suggests a large number of worthwhile specific projects. Includes comments by other experts, e.g., Katona, Simon, etc.

BRADY, ROBERT A. *Business as a System of Power*. New York, Columbia University Press, 1943. A tendentious and one-sided interpretation of the power of big business and business associations. This book is nonetheless useful because of the vigor with which a particular point of view is set out and because of the information assembled on trade associations.

BRAYFIELD, ARTHUR, and WALTER H. CROCKETT. "Employee Attitudes and Employee Performance," *Psychological Bulletin*, Vol. 52, No. 2, 1955. A comprehensive summary and critical analysis of studies of satisfaction and the psychological foundations on which they are based. A professional analysis, and the best summary at its date.

CARTWRIGHT, DORWIN, and ALVIN ZANDER (eds.). *Group Dynamics*. Evanston, Ill., Row, Peterson and Co., 1953. A collection of statements of the principles and some findings of the group dynamic school; not all of them related specifically to industry, but the general threads are important and readable.

CHAMBERLAIN, NEIL. *A General Theory of Economic Process*. New York, Harper and Bros., 1955. A re-interpretation of economic theory as social process, with a strong emphasis on the role and importance of bargaining relations.

CHAPANIS, ALPHONSE, WENDELL R. GARNER, and CLIFFORD MORGAN. *Applied Experimental Psychology*. New York, John Wiley and Sons, 1949. The basic human engineering book, outlining the psychological problems in the design of equipment for human use, problems of measurement, and some illustrations of actual solutions.

DAHL, ROBERT A., and CHARLES E. LINDBLOM. *Politics, Economics and Welfare*. New York, Harper and Bros., 1953. An attempt to integrate certain aspects of economic theory and political science. Planning and politico-economic systems are resolved into basic social processes.

DOWNS, ANTHONY. *An Economic Theory of Democracy*. New York, Harper and Bros., 1957. A bold effort to explain party and electoral competition, voting behavior, etc. with a model using axioms and propositions drawn from economics.

DRUCKER, PETER F. *The Concept of the Corporation*. New York, The John Day Co., 1946. The author, a professional political scientist, studied General Motors for eighteen months. He views the modern corporation as a political institution.

DUBIN, ROBERT. *World of Work*. Englewood Cliffs, N.J., Prentice-Hall, Inc., 1958. A good example of the half-dozen existing texts on industrial sociology. Has a rich bibliography and skillfully integrates the findings of a large number of empirical studies.

EDWARDS, WARD. "The Theory of Decision-making," *Psychological Bulletin*, Vol. 51, No. 4, 1954. A comprehensive survey, as of the date, of psychological experiments relevant to economic analysis of utility and expected value.

FAINSOD, MERLE, LINCOLN GORDON, and JOSEPH PALAMOUNTAIN. *Government and the American Economy*. 3rd ed. New York, W. W. Norton and Co., 1959. A new and extensively revised edition of the leading text and reference work in the field. The book covers a wide range of topics, provides a factual survey of the operation of government at almost every point where it touches the economy, and is descriptive rather than theoretical.

FAINSOD, MERLE, "The Study of Government and Economic Life in the United States," in *Contemporary Social Science*. Paris, UNESCO, 1950. A compact summary.

GHISELLI, EDWIN E., and CLARENCE W. BROWN. *Personnel and Industrial Psychology*. New York, McGraw-Hill Book Co., 1948. A comprehensive summary in text-book form of the traditional areas of industrial psychology, including selection, safety, evaluation, and the like; less adequate on social factors.

GORDON, ROBERT AARON, *Business Leadership in the Large Corporation*. Washington, The Brookings Institution, 1945. The most detailed study to date of who the decision-makers are in the large corporations.

HAIRE, MASON (ed.). *Modern Organization Theory*. New York, John Wiley and Sons, 1959. A group of papers by various social scientists, all focused on the problem of organization. No resolution is presented, but the diversity of approach provides a useful breadth.

HAIRE, MASON. *Psychology in Management*. New York, McGraw-Hill Book Co., 1956. An attempt to show the general applicability of psychological theory of motivation, learning, and perception to industrial problems. Written at a level understandable to non-professionals.

KATONA, GEORGE. *Psychological Analysis of Economic Behavior*. New York, McGraw-Hill Book Co., 1951. The author has for many years conducted consumer studies for the Federal Reserve Board, and also interviewed a large number of businessmen on a variety of topics. He summarizes his findings and relates them systematically to contemporary psychological theory.

KATZ, ELIHU, and P. F. LAZARSFELD. *Personal Influence*. Glencoe, Ill., The Free Press, 1955. The first part of this book reviews the literature on small group research and relates it to the available findings on the role and effect of the mass media. The second part reports a specific study, comparing the impact of personal influence and mass media on the buying habits of a sample of mid-western women.

KELLEY, STANLEY, JR. *Professional Public Relations and Political Power.* Baltimore, Johns Hopkins Press, 1956. A concise survey of the growth in professional public relations and four case studies of public relations men at work in particular political campaigns.

KEY, V. O. *Politics, Parties and Pressure Groups.* 4th ed. New York, Thomas Y. Crowell Co., 1958. The standard work on the subject.

KOMAROVSKY, MIRRA (ed.). *Common Frontiers of the Social Sciences.* Glencoe, Ill. The Free Press, 1957. Contains a series of debates where the same topic is discussed by social scientists from different disciplines. Of special importance in the present context is a discussion of factory research seen from the point of view of the economist and the sociologist; the sociological elements in Keynesian Theory and in the theory of labor relations; the function of attitude surveys in economic theory.

LANDSBERGER, HENRY A. *Hawthorne Revisited.* Ithaca, N.Y., Cornell University Press, 1958. The beginning of modern industrial sociology is usually dated with the experiments done by the Western Electric Company, under the direction of Elton Mayo, around 1930. This work has ever since been discussed as to its ideological, methodological, and substantive implications. The present book reviews this discussion in a detailed and balanced way.

LANE, ROBERT E. *The Regulation of Businessmen, Social Conditions of Government Economic Control.* New Haven, Conn., Yale University Press, 1954. An interpretation and analysis of the relations between businessmen and government regulations in the perspective of psychological and social factors. The author emerges with the conclusion that the resistance of businessmen to regulations is explainable more by these factors than economic ones.

LATHAM, EARL. *The Group Basis of Politics, A Study in Basing Point Legislation.* Ithaca, N.Y., Cornell University Press, 1952. The opening section is probably the most succinct statement to be found of the theory that political actions can best be explained by an examination of the role of groups. The rest of the book is a detailed case study of Congressional action on a specific measure.

LAZARSFELD, PAUL F., and MORRIS ROSENBERG (eds.). *The Language of Social Research.* Glencoe, Ill., The Free Press, 1955. A collection of about sixty papers by various authors which gives a good idea of current procedures and problems in social research and methodology. In the present context, the most relevant part is the section on "the empirical study of action" which includes studies of buying habits.

LERNER, DANIEL, and HAROLD D. LASSWELL. *The Policy Sciences, Recent Develop-*

ments in Scope and Method. Stanford, Calif., Stanford University Press, 1951. A comprehensive symposium of original articles covering the scope and focus of the policy sciences, research procedures, and problems of policy integration. The volume includes chapters on the policy orientation, the study of primary groups, national character, culture, probability methods, mathematical models, qualitative measurements, etc., each by a well-known authority in the field.

LIKERT, RENSIS, and SAMUEL P. HAYES (eds.). *Some Applications of Behavioral Research.* UNESCO: Science and Society Series, 1957. A collection of reviews of various areas where social research has been used for practical purposes. In the present context, most instructive are the sections on supervision of workers, on research organizations in industrial companies, and on the role of sociological notions in consumer research.

LINDZEY, GARDNER (ed.). *Handbook of Social Psychology.* Cambridge, Mass., Addison-Wesley, 1954. An encyclopedic and comprehensive overview of the field in 1954. An excellent basic reference for the relevant areas. Some chapters, such as Gibb's on Leadership and Haire's on Industrial Social Psychology, are directly relevant; others, such as the chapter on group problem solving, or on communication, are tangentially but importantly related.

MARCH, JAMES G., and HERBERT A. SIMON. *Organizations.* New York, John Wiley and Sons, 1959. An overview of past organization theories and an attempt to phrase the problem in terms of behavior theory.

MERTON, R. K., L. BROOM, and L. COTTRELL (eds.). *Sociology Today.* New York, Basic Books, 1959. The best existing survey of the work done by contemporary sociologists in a large variety of fields. In the present context, most relevant are the sections on organizational analysis and the study of occupations. But many other sections contain material of importance to the student of business.

MILLER, GEORGE A. *Language and Communication.* New York, McGraw-Hill Book Co., 1951. A particular approach to the psychological problems in communication. Heavily weighted with information theory, but a useful book on the general problem.

MILLER, WILLIAM (ed.). *Men In Business.* Cambridge, Mass., Harvard University Press, 1952. A typical selection of the kind of work sponsored by the Harvard Research Center in entrepreneurial history. Contains biographies of individual entrepreneurs, statistics on businessmen in various periods, and analytical discussions of specific historical situations.

ROSENBERG, BERNARD, and DAVID M. WHITE (eds.). *Mass Culture.* Glencoe, Ill., The Free Press, 1957. An example of the complicated issues which arise if the social impact of modern business is seriously discussed. About thirty authors analyze the impact of the mass communication industries (television, movies, magazines, etc.) on American culture. The contributions are organized along a continuum from alarmed criticism to defense of the existing situation.

SELZNICK, PHILIP. *Leadership in Administration.* Evanston, Ill., Row, Peterson and Co., 1957. An insightful discussion of the role of leadership in setting the goals of organizations and adapting them to changing external circumstances. Looks at organizations as social systems with a tendency to self-preservation, and thus continues and enlarges the intellectual tradition which was started by the writings of Chester Barnard and Herbert Simon.

STAGNER, ROSS. *Psychology of Industrial Conflict.* New York, John Wiley and Sons, 1956. An approach through attitudes and perception to the relation between labor and management; analysis of dual allegiance, motives on each side, tactics, and goals.

STEVENS, S. S. (ed.). *Handbook of Experimental Psychology.* New York, John Wiley and Sons, 1951. In many places an unduly technical review of the state of affairs by fields. Many chapters are completely outside the scope of this bibliography, but some, such as Fitts' on "Engineering Psychology and Equipment Design," are particularly appropriate. In general, a basic source at the date of issue.

STONE, C. P. (ed.). *Annual Review of Psychology.* Vols. 1–10. Stanford, Calif., 1950–1959. An annual overview by fields of developments in psychology. The chapter on industrial psychology is, of course, particularly relevant, but other fields —motivation, learning, social behavior, and the like —are related to the study of business.

TRUMAN, DAVID B. *The Governmental Process.* New York, A. A. Knopf, 1951. One of the most influential works in recent political science. The author sets out an interest-group theory of politics and then examines the American political system in detail from this perspective.

VITELES, MORRIS. *Motivation and Morale in Industry.* New York, W. W. Norton and Co., 1953. The Dean of American industrial psychology reviews the general literature relating to motivation and morale in connection with productivity. Well documented, with much of the original data given.

WALKER, CHARLES R., and ROBERT N. GUEST. *The Man on the Assembly Line* Cambridge, Mass., Harvard University Press, 1952. A very readable report of a survey of attitudes of workers on an assembly line. Insightful, stimulating, and yet immediately related to the data collected.

WASSERMAN, PAUL, and FRED S. SILANDER. *Decision-making: An Annotated Bibliography.* Ithaca, N.Y., Cornell University Press, 1958.

Index